Undercover Investigation 2nd Edition

J. KIRK BAREFOOT

With a Foreword by
V.A. LEONARD, PH.D.
*Professor Emeritus
Department of Police Administration
Washington State University
Pullman, Washington*

BUTTERWORTHS
Boston ● London

Library of Congress Cataloging in Publication Data

Barefoot, J. Kirk.
    Undercover investigation.

    Bibliography: p.
    Includes index.
    1. Undercover operations. I. Title
HV8080.U5B37   1983   363.2'32   82-14704
ISBN 0-409-95076-9

Published by Butterworth Publishers
10 Tower Office Park
Woburn, MA 01801

10 9 8 7 6 5 4 3 2 1

Printed in the United States of America

Contents

About the Author

J. Kirk Barefoot, C.P.P., is Director, Risk Management, for Cluett, Peabody & Co., a multi-facility apparel manufacturing and retailing company headquartered in New York City.

Previously he was Director of Security for Foremost-McKesson, New York-based wholesale drug firm.

The author's interest in the security field and undercover operations in particular was kindled when he worked with a military intelligence team in the Philippines. Headed by the famed army insurgency experts Colonel Wendell Fertig and Major Joseph Rice, the group operated undercover in central Luzon, evaluating the strength and potential of the communist led Hukbalahp (Huks).

Following this service with Air Force intelligence, Mr. Barefoot earned a B.S. in police science and administration at Washington State University.

A frequent speaker on the subjects of internal theft investigation, undercover and the polygraph, Mr. Barefoot is the author of *Employee Theft Investigation* (1979) and editor and principal author of *The Polygraph Story* (1974).

He is past president of the American Polygraph Association and a member of the American Society for Industrial Security, Special Agents Association and National Law Enforcement Associates. He has served as a member of the Security World Awards Committee since 1971.

Foreword

This book belongs in the top desk drawer of every individual involved in the undercover process. Its wealth of "how-to" information for immediate use today and tonight, in the present case and the next one, underscores its role as an indispensable tool in the arsenal of the investigator.

Undercover Investigation likewise belongs in the personal library of the multiplied tens of thousands of police officers who patrol the streets and alleys of the cities and communities in this country around the clock, twenty-four hours a day. Much of the police work from day to day is undercover related. It has been said that the value of a police officer to his department can be measured to an important degree by the nature and extent of his lines of information. Sources of information are the lifeline in this branch of the public service. Among the comments Chief August Vollmer reserved for the new recruit was the admonition, "See all, hear all, say nothing."

In commercial and industrial security, and in military service, undercover investigation assumes a high level of importance. It has to be that way. It is fortunate indeed, that J. Kirk Barefoot has now made available the second edition of *Undercover Investigation*, with its up-to-date coverage of developments that have crossed the field since the appearance of the first edition. As director of risk management and security for Cluett, Peabody & Co., Inc., he is eminently qualified for the assignment.

In addition, this new volume will serve an important purpose as a test and reference work in police training academies, departmental training schools, and police training at the university level.

Barefoot has done it again, with another important contribution to the literature in this very specialized area of investigation.

V.A. Leonard, Ph.D.

Preface

The objective of this text is to provide the security administrator
or law enforcement official with a reference source which can
serve as a guideline in establishing an ongoing undercover operation. More importantly, it is hoped that the book can serve as a
training manual for the new undercover agent and as refresher
material for the experienced agent. The need for such a text
definitely exists in the investigative field. There is actually a
dearth of published material on undercover work. The publica-
tions that do exist on this subject deal almost exclusively with
short-term undercover assignments, those which are common in
making "buys" of narcotics, counterfeit money, or other contraband. Although similar, the techniques involved in this kind of
activity are designed primarily for the buy and not for long-term
infiltration of the criminal gang. Cover stories are designed to
withstand only a cursory type inspection—certainly not the
intense scrutiny one must expect in the long-term assignment.

Since publication of the first edition of this text, many investigative agencies have expanded their training programs for prospective undercover agents. Furthermore, there has been a general
recognition of the importance of accuracy in report writing and
an understanding of entrapment on the part of agents. Labor
arbitrators and many judges have become even more strict on
their interpretation of the rule as to where roping leaves off and

entrapment begins. For this reason, chapters on these issues have been expanded and updated in this edition.

Being mindful that to both corporations and security agencies the position of undercover operative is an entry-level one, I have expanded the text to touch on other areas where the new recruit is apt to become involved in the early stages of his security career. Namely, it is obvious that many surveillance jobs, as well as shopping investigations, are performed by the same young people who are often recruited to do undercover work. Therefore, an effort is made to familiarize the student with some of the aspects of this collateral work so common to the young investigator.

In a recent seminar, the head of an undercover security agency stated that 50 percent of his agency's successful theft cases was made by approximately six members of the undercover staff, although his staff of undercover agents was approximately triple that number. He further stated that one of the six agents had never failed to make a significant theft case regardless of what assignment had been given to him. It just seemed that wherever this agent was sent, he was able to work his way into the confidence of the people and produce a case. This is not meant to imply that the other agents were incompetent; rather, that they were not as good at roping and probably made their cases using longer and more circuitous methods.

When Mr. Harry Lindberg first came to work for me, fresh out of Michigan State University Police Administration School, he was given a general briefing as well as a briefing on his first assignment. One of the statements I made to Mr. Lindberg was that after several assignments, he would develop that sixth sense which is peculiar to all good undercover agents. He was told that his later cases would be put together more rapidly than the initial ones, and that, eventually, by entering a company distribution center and simply walking through, he would be able to tentatively pick out approximately 50 percent of the hard-core thieves employed on the payroll. This was completely contrary to anything that Mr. Lindberg had been taught, and he certainly was not ready to accept such an apparently wild and frivolous statement. However, today, Harry Lindberg regularly teaches this concept to his students in undercover training classes. We have seen this statement come true time and time again with the development of outstanding undercover agents. On a number of occasions, after successful interrogations, security managers have asked a confessed company thief how he first became involved in collusion with another company employee. The response has often been something along these lines, "I looked at him and he looked at me, and we both knew we could make a deal."

The above points illustrate the essence of good undercover work. Why are some agents always successful and, by the same token, why are other agents never successful? Some recruits have it in the beginning, others develop it, while others never do. It is this "sixth sense" that this edition purports to hone and further develop.

Acknowledgements

Mr. Harry S. Lindberg, Security Systems Manager for Foremost-McKesson, Inc. was to have been a coauthor of this book. Because of personal reasons, he was forced to withdraw during the discussion phases of the text. Nevertheless, I am deeply indebted to Harry Lindberg for his many ideas and suggestions which were incorporated. Mr. Lindberg was the agent involved in many of the case examples and consequently is responsible for many of the philosophies and concepts of undercover work as presented herein.

Last, but not least, acknowledgment must be given to Dr. V.A. Leonard, author of the Foreword to this book. It was Dr. Leonard who first proposed the idea of this book and encouraged its beginning.

J.K.B.

1

Historical Background and Present-Day Usage

Undercover work, as we know it today, must surely have had its origin in military campaigns. In our own history, we can find examples of military intelligence work going back to the Revolutionary War. The American colonies benefited from the talents of the great patriot, Nathan Hale; while on the British side, the exploits of John Andre have been given proper attention in history books. During the Civil War, we certainly must recognize the accomplishments of Belle Boyd for the South and of course Allen Pinkerton[1] for the North. World War I cannot be reviewed without mentioning the infamous Mata Hari. In World War II we found more sophisticated intelligence gathering and undercover activities, which were noted by the terms "fifth column" and "espionage." The activities of the American Office of Strategic Services must also be recognized.

---

[1] Allen Pinkerton and the Pinkerton family played a large part in the settling of the western states of the country after the Civil War and, in particular, handling security for not only the government but also the railroads. Agents for this era were commonly referred to as "Pinkertons." The outgrowth of this activity was the founding of the Pinkerton Detective Agency, generally conceded to be the largest of the national private agencies. The agency has continued in the tradition of intelligence gathering and regularly offers undercover service to many industrial clients throughout the United States.

The spotlight of the post-World War II era brought into focus the activities of such people as the Russian Colonel Rudolph Abel and Matt Cevetic,[2] a famous undercover agent in the Federal Bureau of Investigation (FBI) who infiltrated the Communist party; also of course, the seldom acknowledged, but often speculated, activities of the Central Intelligence Agency (CIA). The basic difference between the work of these many people or groups and present-day undercover agents is one of semantics. Military operatives are called "spies"—a word which sometimes connotes a "dirty business" type of activity. In industrial security and law enforcement, we have attempted to give some measure of respectability to intelligence gathering people calling them "undercover agents" or "undercover operatives." Regardless of terms, the name of the game is basically the same—a deep penetration and a gathering of information on the opposition or the enemy.

LAW ENFORCEMENT

Undercover has been used by law enforcement agencies to varying degrees in the past. One of the earliest uses was the infiltration of train robber gangs by Pinkerton agents following the Civil War. In recent years the public has become aware of undercover operations which have come about because of specific situations in a particular locale. From time to time, various crime commissions, for instance, will recruit an experienced investigator from another city to work in an undercover capacity and infiltrate a suspected allegiance between local politicians and organized crime. A number of the more progressive police departments such as Los Angeles, Chicago, and New York have long maintained

---

[2] Cevetic was recruited and coached by the FBI to infiltrate the Communist party of Pennsylvania in the Pittsburgh district during the 1940s. As a result of his many years as an FBI undercover agent, certain leaders within the party were prosecuted by the State of Pennsylvania in what was probably the first and only sedition trial ever conducted by one of the states of the Union. The trial was prosecuted by the then assistant district attorney of Allegheny County, Pennsylvania, Gilbert Helwig. Helwig, at this writing, is serving as a trial attorney for the prestigious law firm of Reed, Smith, Shaw, and McClay in Pittsburgh, Pennsylvania. Cevetic's exploits have been well documented in his book, *The Big Decision* (1959).

intelligence units with the sole responsibility of gathering information in connection with the local elements of the organized crime structure. There is little question that a sizable percentage of the total information developed by these units has come about through the efforts of police officers working in an undercover capacity. Although less formalized, for many years it has been the practice of most police departments in metropolitan areas to assign rookie patrolmen, upon graduation from the local police academy, to work in the vice division in an undercover capacity. Members of organized crime in any locale, along with the local gambling operators and prostitutes, make it their business to become acquainted with and get to know the faces of as many members of the police department as possible. Because of this, the new rookie patrolman is always in demand for undercover assignments in the vice and narcotics units. In the narcotics unit, in order to make a case, it is necessary to make "buys."

Some of the more long-term undercover activities in local law enforcement have come into sharp focus recently because of the need for police agencies to infiltrate revolutionary groups such as the Black Panthers and other radical organizations which are dedicated to violence, disruption of law and order, or the overthrow of government processes. In the Black Panther trials in New York, the undercover assignments ran several years.

Police undercover operations in the late 1970s were often described by the media as "sting" operations. Generally, local or state police would open up in a vacant storefront or warehouse and pose as professional "fences" or buyers of stolen goods. Over a period of many months, the police working in such an undercover capacity would purchase large amounts of contraband from thieves and other criminals who would just wander in. The business grew by word of mouth and encouraged repeat visits by the criminal element. Over a period of time, the police would generally gather together enough physical and other evidence to eventually spring the trap and round up all the criminals involved. This operation was worked in many cities across the United States and seemed to be in vogue for some time. No doubt, the criminal population has begun to become extremely wary of dealing with fences who do not have the proper credentials.

The most recent example of law enforcement's use of undercover operations was the revelation of the so-called abscam operations in 1980 and 1981. As a result of these undercover efforts, the FBI was able to obtain successful prosecutions on a number of governmental figures, including congressmen and one senator, along with a number of private attorneys. The key undercover agent in each of these cases has been described by the media as the government's chief informant, Mel Weinberg. A close study of each of the cases reveals that their success hinged on Weinberg's ability to rope the suspects. Defense attorneys maintained that Weinberg's efforts at roping constituted entrapment, but the government successfully overcame this contention in the trials. Therefore it can be assumed that entrapment, in the legal sense, did not play a major role in any of the investigative efforts.

GOVERNMENT AND MILITARY SERVICES

Intelligence has always been given a very healthy priority by all the major military services. Intelligence gathering in the Navy comes under the office of Naval Investigations Services Organization (NISO). In the Air Force, it is included in the activities of the Office of Special Investigations (OSI), and in the Army it has usually been a function of the G-2 Section. Although actual undercover operations are probably more commonplace in the Army, there is little question that all military services have engaged at one time or another in undercover operations. It is to be noted that in order to combat or counter the activities of undercover agents of another power, the Army has developed a unit called the Counter Intelligence Corps. Both the Navy and the Air Force have people engaged in comparable activity.

The biggest civilian-operated intelligence gathering unit today is of course the CIA. Probably unlike its sister agencies, the National Security Agency (NSA) and the Army Security Agency (ASA), the CIA engages in a great deal of undercover activities on a worldwide basis. Although science has developed many sophisticated electronic products to aid in intelligence gathering, there still remains no substitute for the agent who works undercover.

Our number one domestic antiespionage agency of course is the FBI. Unlike many other federal government agencies, the FBI, according to reliable sources, has always relied more on paid informants and recruitment from outside the ranks rather than assigning its own special agents to work in an undercover capacity. Examples of successful undercover operatives who were recruited by the FBI from the outside were Matt Cevetic and Herbert A. Philbrick.[3] The federal law enforcement agency which is held in highest esteem for its undercover accomplishments is the old Federal Bureau of Narcotics.[4] This agency's expertise on undercover work has come about by the very nature of the cases which are handled by the Bureau of Narcotics, rather than any particular leaning toward this type of investigative approach. Narcotics undercover agents have frequently been loaned to other federal law enforcement agencies throughout the years. This is because the average Treasury agent, Secret Service agent, or FBI agent runs to a definite type and just would not have the proper mental attitude or even physical appearance to be successful in infiltrating an underworld gang. Many narcotic and drug agents, on the other hand, seem to be selected for their physical appearance which lends itself to successful undercover work. As an example, one of my own undercover agents had the classic "textbook" appearance of a drug addict. Eventually he resigned to accept a position with the Federal Bureau of Narcotics and became a very successful undercover agent for that agency.

BUSINESS AND INDUSTRY

The reader may be surprised to learn that, outside of government service, the vast majority of undercover agents are not found in law enforcement activities but in business and industry. A sizable number of these men and women are employed directly by corporations for internal investigation, but most are employed by private agencies. Companies and corporations are their clients, and the agency undercover man performs investigative work

---

[3] Herbert A. Philbrick was another anti-Communist agent who successfully infiltrated the U.S. Communist party. This was documented in a television series entitled "I Led Three Lives."

[4] The Federal Bureau of Narcotics, formerly a part of the United States Treasury Department, was merged with the Bureau of Drug Abuse Control (BDAC) in 1968. The new agency, which has been placed within the Justice Department, is now known as the Drug Enforcement Administration (DEA).

for them. This situation has come about because of the devastating impact of crime on American business.

One source (Walsh and Healy, 1974) estimates U.S. business losses for robbery, burglary, theft, embezzlement, and fraud at $5 billion annually. This same authority states that 30 percent of all business bankruptcies are caused by employee dishonesty. Another source (U.S. Department of Commerce, 1975) states that crimes against business and industry are running at a minimum of $23.6 billion a year. Of this amount, the American Management Association estimated that between $5 billion and $10 billion in losses are believed caused by employee pilferage. The difficulty in arriving at an accurate figure comes about because many companies are reluctant to file fidelity claims with their insurance carriers. Most companies carry fidelity insurance to be used only in the case of a defalcation that would amount to corporate disaster. Costs of most fidelity insurance are determined in such a way that frequent claims, even though provable, ultimately result in higher premiums; thus, the employer pays the entire bill in the end. In addition, a sizable percentage of thefts within business and industry go completely undetected and are not reported simply because they are never discovered.

Security Letter, in its February 16, 1982, issue, points out that the U.S. Department of Commerce, American Management Association, and the U.S. Chamber of Commerce are no longer collecting information which would tend to pinpoint crime against industry or the total amount of employee theft. *Security Letter* also points out that it is possible to extrapolate from the above figures for current years, by using the population increase of 5.7 percent from 1975 to 1980. During this same period, the FBI's Crime Index rose 18.1 percent, of which 17 percent was nonviolent incidents. At this same time, the Consumer Price Index (CPI) rose 53.1 percent. *Security Letter* suggests multiplying the 1975 estimates by the increase in the total crime index for this period of time, multiplied by the CPI, to convert losses to 1980 dollars.

The publication is quick to point out that this method of estimate is shaky at best. It assumes that all business crimes increase the same percentage as crime as a whole, which is a risky assumption. Also, the assumption that the CPI is a satisfactory multiplier to convert the value of 1975 business losses into those of 1981 may also be risky. As an example, *Security Letter* illustrates that using the above formula arson losses would leap from $1.3 billion to $2.3 billion. However, the National Fire Protection Association estimates arson losses in 1980 at only $1.76 billion. This, of course, is high, but is far less than the estimate obtained through the suggested formula.

From my own experience, officials of McKesson & Robbins, Inc.[5] at a company conference at the Shamrock Hotel in Houston, Texas, December 1959, announced to the assembled audience that their best estimate of loss due to internal theft within the company was over $1 million per year. This was on a sales volume of approximately $650 million per year. After a series of successful undercover cases over the next six years, officials of the company acknowledged in 1967 that internal theft within the corporation had been reduced to somewhere in the neighborhood of $250,000 annually on a sales volume which had increased to $1 billion a year.

Because of the volume of theft that exists today in American business and industry, undercover departments of the old-line private detective agencies are flourishing. New agencies, specializing in undercover work exclusively, have sprung up and are now enjoying a sizable portion of the undercover business.

PRIVATE AGENCIES AND COMPANY UNDERCOVER MEN

As mentioned earlier, most of the industrial undercover operatives are employed by either agencies specializing in undercover work or the more conventional old-line detective agencies. For the reader who might be contemplating retaining such an agency for undercover work, it would seem only fair to mention a few of the more prominent agencies. Organizations along with their principal and executive office locations specializing in undercover and

---

[5] McKesson & Robbins, Inc., formerly the nation's largest wholesaler, ceased to exist as a corporation in July of 1967 when it was merged with Foremost Dairies. The successor corporation is known as Foremost-McKesson, Inc.

operating on a nationwide basis are: Management Safeguards, New York City (Saul Astor); Investigation, Inc., New York City (Norman Jaspen); Lincoln Controls, New York City (Max Binder). Three of the largest conventional private detective agencies that operate undercover departments are Burns International Security Services, Inc., Briarcliff Manor, New York; Pinkerton Detective Agency, Inc., New York City; Wackenhut Agency, Coral Gables, Florida.

There are of course other very competent organizations offering undercover service. Often a strictly local agency will have much more capability and know-how in a particular location than would an organization operating on a nationwide basis. The mark of quality in industrial undercover work is the ability of the undercover man himself plus the quality of his supervision. These two factors determine the success of the investigation.

In recent years, a number of large companies have developed their own undercover investigative staff. Before embarking on such a venture, there are a number of factors that must be taken into consideration. A company working on a do-it-yourself basis cannot compete with the agency in diversity and flexibility of personnel. Does the position call for an accountant, an engineer, a teacher, a pilot, or some other professional person? If so, most agencies have these people on tap; if not, they have methods of recruiting the necessary help. Agencies are also able to make substitutions of personnel when the need arises, as it occasionally does. Other agency advantages may be better training and supervision. Unless a company has the professional skill necessary for training and supervision, it would be disastrous to attempt to engage in its own undercover efforts.

With all the agency advantages that have been enumerated, why should a company even consider its own undercover staff? The first answer, and the biggest, is economy. For a four-week job where the worker's salary is $175 per week, the agency may charge from $1,000 up—over and above the ordinary wages paid to the operative. On a do-it-yourself basis, the same four week's work might cost about $1,000 in salary, from which the $175 per week or $700 would act to offset the $1,000, leaving a net cost of $300 for the four-week effort. Of course, a company does not get off quite this easily. To this must be added costs of moving expenses from one city to another plus salary and expenses while engaged in setting up a proper cover. Table 1.1 illustrates this point. The key is that the agent is presumed carried on a corporate payroll and that the local wages earned ($700) is deducted monthly from his corporate salary.

The reader should be able to visualize the tremendous difference in cost. A number of companies over the years have tried agency personnel and became so dissatisfied as to sour on the whole concept of undercover. In all fairness, however, not all the blame can be laid at the doorstep of the agency. This can be illustrated with the experience of McKesson & Robbins, Inc.

When the McKesson security department was formed in 1954, it was headed by a retired Secret Service agent, Frank Seckler. Seckler had spent most of his twenty-some years with the government doing undercover work—not only for the Secret Service, but also on loan to other Treasury enforcement agencies from time to time. He had become the most famous and successful undercover man in the history of the U.S. government. His

TABLE 1.1   Comparative Costs of Agency and In-House Undercover Work

Item	In-House	Agency	Remarks
Base salary per month	$1,300	$1,000	Agency charge to client per month
Local salary	− 700	+ 700	
Net	600	1,700	Base outlay by company
Monthly incidental expenses	60	60	
Subtotal	660	1,760	
	None	75	Living subsidy if agent is from out of town
Subtotal	660	1,835	
Relocation expense, maximum and prorated monthly based on two relocates per year	175	50	Relocation if from out of town, prorated
	835		
Cover expense prorated	50		
Total	$ 885	$1,885	May be minimum only

exploits were serialized by newspaper chains upon his retirement. Without question, he knew the business as no one else did.

After joining McKesson, Seckler made an early attempt to infiltrate suspected company theft rings by hiring agency personnel. In most cases the results were unsatisfactory and the agency's services were terminated. When I was appointed director of security at the company in 1958 upon Seckler's death, I studied these failures closely to determine the reasons and came up with the following conclusions:

1. Seckler himself was a highly trained perfectionist, and agency personnel just did not measure up to his own abilities.
2. Agency costs—even in the period 1954 to 1957—were high. Being a wholesaler, McKesson was extremely cost conscious and this pressure would begin to build within several weeks. This, in turn, created a false expectation of results within at least thirty days.
3. The company's new security controls worked against undercover and completely ruled out the possibility of an early break within thirty days.
4. Most agency personnel did not take a personal interest in the case—for some, it was just another in a long series of assignments.
5. Many agency operatives were on their first case and had only a minimum of training and orientation. They were given printed instructions on what to look for and what to report. They had no coaching on the art of roping, and in some cases their reports were given verbally to an agency "rewrite man" who then "composed" the report for the day.

Based on these findings, a new plan was submitted to top management—one that was to prove itself practical in case after case. It was a new concept in undercover work: company undercovermen.

Management had to be educated to a new concept of long-term undercover investigation. No longer would the company move against an individual thief exposed in the first thirty days or so of the undercover investigation. They were now constrained to accept the theory that internal theft in a company is like a cancer. Every vestige must be exposed during any investigation in order that the cancer may be eliminated or controlled. To apprehend only several thieves among dozens certainly never cures the problem. At best only a temporary deterrent effect can be expected, following which the thieves become more sophisticated and cautious in their theft activities. Furthermore, the techniques used by security managers in both the undercover phase and the "bust" phase may well be a one-shot effort, just as the cancer surgeon may only be given one opportunity at major and radical surgery. Experience showed that an average industrial undercover case lasted six months. In most instances it took three months for the agent to gain full acceptance by the workers. The remaining three months could then be devoted to building his case—one which would stand up and which would give the interrogators an overwhelming advantage over the suspects during the bust.

2

Selection and Recruitment of Undercover Personnel

LOCAL LAW ENFORCEMENT

The problem of recruitment of undercover officers for the large metropolitan police department is usually one that can be handled within the capabilities of the department itself. Large metropolitan centers such as New York, Chicago, Los Angeles, and others should have no difficulty in selecting the correct type of undercover officers from the various ethnic and racial backgrounds which are represented within any recruit class graduating from the local police academy. Many rookie patrolmen actually look forward to the opportunity of joining an undercover squad either within the narcotics division or vice squad. The more hazardous, long-term undercover assignment which usually is involved in subversive infiltration more properly calls for volunteers rather than the arbitrary assignment of some of the short-term undercover jobs.

With proper manpower planning, availability of undercover officers from within state police organizations should be entirely practical. Although not necessarily large in terms of total manpower, any state police organization has one advantage over any local law enforcement agency in that it is statewide. Thus it is able to bring in trained undercover officers from other geographical sections of the state to a troubled area where they could operate effectively.

The main problem of undercover availability for the moderately sized and small municipal departments and also for local sheriff's offices is one of narrow geographic confines along with limited manpower. The only obvious solution to those smaller departments, which could normally only engage in the briefest of undercover assignments, would be to provide sufficient funds in each annual budget for the payment of outside undercover service. In this case, it is possible that competent undercover officers could be obtained on loan from the state police or from another local department. If this were not possible, then, as has been the case many times, the local department should be able to contract with a private agency for the specific undercover type which is needed. As mentioned earlier, the private agency would have a definite advantage in being able to supply the exact type of individual required for a specific assignment. Such a latitude in selection might not always be available, even when considering a loan of an officer from another department. Many times, personnel available from a private agency would obviously not be physically able to meet basic police qualifications. This obvious difference in size and outward appearance automatically lends some degree of immunity to suspicion on the part of the underworld.

PRIVATE AGENCIES

Surprisingly enough, most undercover operatives who are employed by private agencies are found to have been recruited through newspaper advertisements. Naturally, any private agency prefers an undercover operative with prior experience. However, this is not always possible, so that the private agency is often forced to hire individuals without any type of investigative training, which the agency must provide. In my experience, most undercover personnel who are retained by agencies have, at best, a high school education. Very few operatives, with the exception of some technicians or specialists, have ever had any college or university training. What few do have formal educational training beyond high school are not kept on undercover assignments by the agency more than a year or so. They invariably end up in supervisory positions within the undercover department or are transferred to management training programs within other departments of the agency. A considerable number of agency undercover personnel are not even high school graduates, and therefore they have built-in deficiencies that must be recognized and coped with by their supervisor. A surprising number of these people with little formal education are extremely adept in the art of roping. On the other hand, it is often the case that those with more of a formal education find the art of roping extremely difficult to master and are forced to pursue their undercover assignment simply through their powers of observation and deductive reasoning.

COMPANY UNDERCOVER MEN

A number of companies that have attempted undercover operations on their own have simply used the same basic recruiting techniques as are in use by most private agencies. Consequently, these companies attempt to employ undercover agents with prior experience from the agencies. Few, if any, of the companies recruiting in this manner have any sort of a comprehensive training program and are dependent upon the experienced operative. On the other hand, a number of national corporations with security departments have attempted recruitment of their undercover staffs from colleges and universities. These schools offer two- and four-year programs in police administration and industrial security. McKesson & Robbins recruited investigators for undercover work from schools such as Washington State University, Michigan State University, Indiana State University of Pennsylvania, San Jose State College, Fresno State College, Arizona State University, University of Arizona, New Mexico State College, and Florida State University. All in all, there are dozens that number of colleges and universities offering either two- or four-year programs in law enforcement subjects at this time. In recruiting from these sources, the corporate security executive is often able to attract graduating seniors, who, because of physical limitations such as height, weight, and eyesight would not be accepted by either a local department or a federal law enforcement agency.

The following list illustrates some of the common differences between young people who are fresh out of criminal justice programs and the typical experienced operative from the street (Barefoot, 1979).

Agency Operative	*Police Science Graduate*
1. Usually good at roping. (See explanation below.)	1. May be poor at roping.
2. May not know legal aspects of the work.	2. Usually has insight into legal considerations.
3. May be a poor report writer, necessitating a rewrite man.	3. Can usually write acceptable reports.
4. Sometimes makes a poor to fair impression on judge or jury.	4. Usually comes across as a professional in court.
5. Usually blends in and is street wise.	5. May not blend in and is straight.

These comparisons are certainly not meant to be absolute, but rather are factors that occur at a rate greater than chance. Most deficiencies can be corrected through adequate training; even the lack of formal college education can be offset by training and experience. Although a large company may be able to hire police science graduates, without question the only sensible route for the smaller company is to use agency operatives. Several large corporate security departments successfully use both.

By offering career opportunities in security, the corporate security department can often attract graduating police science seniors who would prove a valuable addition to any security operation. A proper on-the-job training program, with periodic advancement, must be laid out in advance for the average person with a college background of this type. The usual graduating senior is either single or newly married, and thus can offer four to five years of periodic undercover work to a corporate security department. After this time, there are usually children of school age in the family, and then the security executive must be prepared to reassign his undercover investigator to a more permanent and stable security position. By interspersing undercover assignments with other investigative assignments such as tail jobs, surveillances, background and street type investigations, and other security work, the security executive keeps the monotony and boredom of the undercover assignments to a minimum. In this approach he is not only maintaining the morale of his college-trained undercover agent, he is also giving him valuable experience in other areas of the security field in preparation for the day when he can be moved out of undercover work and into an open security assignment.

One word of caution is in order: Many police science students, because of their family backgrounds and upbringing, are never able to adapt successfully to undercover work. They find the art of roping difficult, if not impossible, to master. On the other hand, if the security recruiter is selective, he will attempt to recruit his potential undercover agent from a middle- or lower-class background, one who has had some job experience such as truck driver, laborer, dock worker, stock clerk, or janitor. Also, the more education the candidate has had in the "school of hard knocks" the better his chances of success as an undercover agent. The one major drawback, in addition to those already enumerated in recruiting from the police science colleges, is the availability, or rather the scarcity, of police science students from minority groups. What few police science students there are who are either black or of Spanish heritage are in great demand by the federal law enforcement agencies such as the Drug Enforcement Administration. Competition for these students is very keen indeed, and the corporate executive able to land graduating police science majors from a minority group should feel fortunate indeed.

Finally, the corporate executive should not overlook the possibility of recruitment from within the ranks of present employees. Although this is not recommended generally, occasionally it has proved successful and on occasion the only answer to infiltration.

SCREENING THE UNDERCOVER CANDIDATE

In addition to normal personnel screening devices such as the physical examination and IQ test, two tests of great importance to selection of undercover personnel are a psychological questionnaire to determine the existence of a normal psychological profile and also a test on memory or retentive powers. It is mandatory that the undercover candidate be free of any abnormal traits such as severe anxieties, excessive irritability, evasiveness, and any other psychological abnormalities that would work against a successful undercover endeavor. Because many an undercover investigation is built around a collection of minute and seemingly insignificant facts, coupled with the investigator's inability to take notes on the spot, an unusual memory or retentive powers that are particularly attuned to names, faces, identifying marks, description, and so forth are a practical necessity. There is at least one good written test available to measure memory.[1]

The most critical test for an undercover candidate, however, is probably the most unusual, the polygraph screening examination. Because of the serious questions of morality that are raised by the prospect of entrapment in any undercover assignment, and also because of the techniques that are necessary in the art of successful roping, polygraph examination prior to employment is an absolute must. In the case of police undercover personnel, it is also highly desirable; and in fact each year that passes sees more and more police departments across the country turn to polygraph screening of police applicants for all types of police jobs. Many industrial undercover cases are never resolved by a thorough investigation and interrogation of suspects at the end of the case such as might be possible in the police field. Consequently, it is not difficult for an overzealous undercover operative to attempt to please his superiors and the clients by entrapping honest fellow employees. In addition, a number of security executives have ultimately discovered that their undercover personnel were just as dishonest, if not more so, than the worst thieves on their payroll. All of these things dictate the selection of a morally sound, honest, and truthful individual for an undercover assignment. The only sure way that such a determination can be made is through a polygraph screening examination administered by a well-trained competent polygraphist. The reader is referred to the American Polygraph Association for a listing of practitioners in his area.[2]

---

[1] Memory Test," Industrial Psychology, Inc., New York, NY 10022.

[2] American Polygraph Association, P.O. Box 74, Linthicum Heights, MD 21090.

Any polygraph examination of an undercover applicant should include questions concerning truthfulness and completeness of the employment application, any arrest record of consequence, dishonesty from former employers, unsolved criminal offenses which may have been committed by the applicant, undisclosed physical disabilities which may be concealed by the applicant, significant use of narcotics or other dangerous drugs, and, in the case of a veteran, any significant military discipline or courts martial. In the case of an applicant with prior experience, questions should be included concerning the reporting and handling of all stolen property utilized by the undercover agent in previous cases to further his roping.

Although I have never favored the general use of the polygraph in periodic screening of employees, in this regard it is felt that periodic screening is not only worthwhile but essential. Because of the problems of entrapment and personal honesty in connection with roping, a policy of periodic polygraph examinations was approved and required by top management of McKesson & Robbins for the undercover staff from its inception in 1958. Generally speaking, each investigator was given a routine screening examination at the conclusion of each of his undercover assignments or approximately every six months.

In those states where polygraph screening of job applicants is not permissible as a condition of employment, an alternative system of fidelity screening is the Reid Report,[3] a written questionnaire which accurately measures attitudes toward honesty.

---

[3] Developed by John E. Reid & Associates in 1950, Chicago. The Reid Report is the original "pencil and paper" test for honesty. It has been refined until its validity and reliability are now accepted by the scientific community.

3

Training

PRIVATE AGENCIES

The problem of training, or rather the lack of it, is probably the largest single factor retarding the growth of industrial undercover services as offered by private agencies. Many are the corporate executives who, over the years, have expressed time and again, "We tried undercover once, and I'd never do it again." There are probably many reasons for such statements to be made, but all can be traced back to a common cause: the lack of formal training given to the new undercover man prior to his assignment.

This is not to say that all industrial undercover personnel employed by agencies are incompetent because of their lack of training. Many of these men, simply by using good judgment and making the most of their experiences over the years, have developed into highly competent agents and would do justice to any security organization fortunate enough to have them on their payroll. Unfortunately, there is not an abundance of people with this competency available. The rate of turnover in most agencies offering undercover services is quite high, and it would be unusual to find many persons on a particular staff with as much as ten years of service. The very nature of the job is such that it leads to a high rate of turnover, and consequently it is quite common to encounter an undercover agent who is working on his first (and possibly last) assignment. The basic philosophy of most security agencies is that payroll costs for security personnel such as undercover, guards, and investigators always should be billed ultimately to a client. There is always a great reluctance on the part of most agencies to carry an employee on the agency payroll for purposes of training, stand-by, and so on. In fact, one of the problems contributing to the high rate of turnover is that many agencies will lay off an undercover person at the conclusion of an assignment if a second assignment is not readily available. Because of this, the average undercover agent simply goes from one agency to another. Consequently good men are not retained on one particular payroll, and incompetent men are able to perpetuate themselves in the industry for a number of years.

When the first edition of this text was being written in the early 1970s, I had occasion to interview a number of undercover agents from various agencies regarding their training. At that time, most training appeared to be minimal and, in some cases, almost nonexistent save for a typewritten sheet of instructions of what to put in their reports. I believe this situation has changed materially in the past ten years. Agencies have now upgraded their training of undercover recruits to go far beyond the printed sheet of instructions. A number of agencies have formalized their training, and in fact, one agency, Management Safeguards, Inc., has prepared training sessions on videotape cassettes. Some agencies have lengthened their training to as much as five days. Unfortunately, many of the smaller local agencies have not upgraded or improved their training programs, so that the industry is still plagued with a significant number of ill-trained undercover operatives.

Many an industrial undercover agent employed by an agency has little or no knowledge of the more important concepts of his work. He has little training or knowledge on how to recognize, mark, and preserve physical evidence of gambling, drugs, merchandise thefts, and so forth. Through experience and instinct, he may well be adept at the art of roping but often knows little or nothing about the rules of entrapment. Compared to a professional in law enforcement, his testimony in court concerning an investigation that he has completed usually is woeful, and he presents an inviting target to the aggressive defense attorney during cross-examination.

Three-fourths of smaller companies and one-half of larger companies have never used an undercover agent (Table 3.1). But among larger companies, undercover agents are used either "periodically" or "often" by 15 percent of the firms (Bureau of National Affairs, 1972). There is little question that if all agencies were able to offer adequately trained undercover agents to business and industry, the rate of use of such services by corporations would increase at least 50 percent over present volume.

It is because of the above weaknesses in the industry that many companies have turned toward developing their own undercover staff. It was through developing such a staff, with the best possible training available at the time, that successes at McKesson were achieved which had never been realized in previous years of dealing with agencies. Furthermore, it was because of these factors that the idea of this text was conceived. It is hoped that this book can serve as the basis for a long step forward on the part of agencies and corporations in their training of undercover agents.

During the 1950s and 1960s, it was common practice for many security executives to rely on their interrogation skills, possibly supplemented by polygraph examinations, to break suspected larceny cases. I know one former security official of a large mail-order house in Chicago who regularly strolled the order-filling and packing departments "looking over" the employees as they went about their tasks. Using that "sixth sense" which is peculiar to many security practitioners, he would settle on a

TABLE 3.1   Use of Undercover Agents

| | Percentage of Companies | | |
	Small	Large	All
Never	76	51	62
Rarely	13	25	20
Periodically	9	12	11
Often	0	3	2
No response	1	9	5

particular employee who did not look "right." After summoning the suspected employee to the security office, the security executive would commence an interrogation that more often than not would result in a confession and signed statement of theft of company property by the employee. Needless to say, there was never any evidence of wrongdoing beforehand, and the whole procedure amounted to little more than a fishing expedition. In those days, even though a company was organized by a labor union, the security chief was under no obligation to provide any union representation during the interrogation of the hapless employee. In fact, the labor laws of those days were quite clear that union representation was not necessary during the investigative phase; it need only be present during a disciplinary action of the employee.

The problem with "cold turkey" interrogation has now become more acute because of a requirement of union representation as set down by the United States Supreme Court (*National Labor Relations Board* v. *J. Weingarten, Inc.*, 1973). All this has resulted in old-fashioned investigative work being necessary before attempting interrogation of suspected union members. In other words, the security executive should have enough of a case beforehand to be able, in the event of an interrogation failure, to take disciplinary action against a suspect and discharge him based on evidence already developed. This brings the pendulum back to one of the basic investigative tools, namely, undercover.

A CORPORATE TRAINING PROGRAM

The undercover training program used at McKesson & Robbins in the early 1960s was set up for in-house use only. In the early 1970s, this training program, which had proved so successful, was sponsored jointly by Foremost-McKesson, Inc., and Cluett, Peabody & Co., Inc. In recent years, every attempt has been made to improve the training program by the production of videotapes concerning drug abuse, roping, and the "burn." Case material has been edited so as to shorten the reading burden upon the student but still retain the essential lessons to be learned.

In 1979, Cluett and Foremost agreed to open the training program, on a nonprofit, break-even basis, to other interested companies that had expressed a desire to participate. This availability to other companies was continued in 1980 and included not only private corporations but some security agencies as well. The training school presently consists of approximately five days instruction including formal classroom lectures, outside reading assignments, and coaching of students on a one-to-one basis. The objective of the training school is not to turn out an experienced undercover agent at the end of five days; rather, the objective is limited to taking the raw recruit and teaching him to think as an undercover agent should think, as well as giving him resources to fall back on and use in the years ahead while working a variety of undercover assignments. For an undercover agent with some experience in the field, but with no formal training, it serves as a finishing school to hone his skills. The philosophy of the school has always acknowledged that experience in the field is the ultimate teacher.

The location of the school is flexible; to date it has been held in moderately priced motels in Chicago, Stamford, Connecticut, and Atlanta, Georgia. The typical student arriving at the school is usually a recent graduate from an industrial security program or a four-year criminal justice department at some college or university. Over the years, the school has enrolled students from such learning institutions as Washington State University, Michigan State University, Northeastern University, Indiana State University, University of Pennsylvania, San Jose State University, and many others. A few of the students have not been college graduates, but have been recruited by their new employer because of special skills that they already possessed. There has also been a sprinkling of security executives in the course, who were intent on developing their own in-house staff and wished to audit the course so as to be able to provide proper supervision to their new undercover recruits. Several agency executives have participated in the course with the intention of setting up their own undercover school on a commercial basis.

Because of the nature of the one-on-one training, the class has been limited to ten students, not counting those persons simply auditing the course. This is handled by two instructors. A third instructor is available for assistance should a class exceed ten students. However, the present maximum of the class would have to be pegged at fifteen.

The students are usually assembled on Sunday evening for a get-acquainted session and also an orientation to the course for the upcoming week. Although the students get to know each other quite well during the week, a number of companies have specifically requested that their company affiliation not be revealed so as not to jeopardize the future cover stories of any of the agents. This is reinforced by the instructors, beginning with the opening session on Sunday evening, and this and similar precautionary measures are constantly reinforced in the student's mind throughout the week.

The student is given hand-out material to orient him to some specialty area such as organized gambling and a copy of *Undercover Investigation* (Barefoot, 1975), which is used as a textbook for the course. This becomes the student's personal property upon completion of the course, as do many other items of training material. Part one of a commercially prepared movie on undercover training is shown on Sunday evening and then the students are given specific reading assignments in the textbook in order to prepare them for the first day's lecture. This advance reading assignment technique, in preparation for the following day's lecture, is used throughout the week.

In addition to the textbook, students are required to read a minimum of six general investigation cases that have been carefully selected and edited so as to possess the greatest educational value. These six cases may be chosen from a total of nine. There are sufficient copies of each case so that there is no waiting time involved, and the faster readers are not hampered by slower readers. In addition to the general investigation cases, students are also required to read one labor arbitration case involving major dishonesty, one federal circuit court of appeals decision on entrapment, and also selected passages of *The Big Decision* (Cevetic, 1959).

The students are required to take notes on the reading of these general cases, the arbitration, court decision, and *The Big Decision*, in order to be able to discuss the cases intelligently with one of the instructors, acting as a trainer, upon completion of each reading assignment. In the general investigation cases, the student is encouraged to project himself mentally into the case and to place himself in the role of the original agent who wrote the reports. He is encouraged to commend the agent when that is indicated, to make constructive criticisms, or to criticize the agent's failures if such is indicated in the report. Each of the general investigation cases has been briefed and a teaching guide prepared for the trainer so that it can be determined, with reasonable certainty, that the student has garnered the important points from the case. Most of the afternoons and evenings during the week are taken up with these special reading assignments. The mornings are generally devoted to specific classroom lectures covering such diverse subjects as:

- History of undercover
- Handling of travel expense reports
- Handling of outside money earned at various jobs
- Claiming reimbursement for working overtime (along with guidelines negotiated years ago with the Wage and Hours section of the Department of Labor)

The student is also lectured on the necessity of periodic polygraph examinations, if such be the policy of the company; how to establish local credit; and how to submit medical claims and handle moving expenses so as not to jeopardize one's cover story.

Other lectures include report writing both as to format and frequency. This particular lecture is supplemented by a practical exercise where the students are sent out of the motel on diverse assignments, then asked to return and write a report. In this way, deficiencies can be spotlighted quickly, and corrective action, if needed, can then be taken.

Further lectures include sessions on drugs in the industrial setting, drinking, gambling, the gathering and marking of evidence, as well as extensive lectures on both roping and entrapment. It is generally conceded that there is often a very fine line of distinction as to where roping ends and entrapment begins. In order to enhance this distinction and to give the student further insight into the art of roping, the textbook is augmented by a reenacted roping scene that has been professionally directed and edited on videotape. On the third day, part two of the commercially prepared undercover training film is shown, as well as demonstrations involving the use of ultraviolet crayons and the so-called black-light.

On the fourth day of the course, a lecture is given on how to build a cover story. The student is also made familiar with the term "staging" in the event that such a procedure should ever be necessary for him during his undercover career. After the lecture on cover stories, the student completes, in detail, a typical employment application and then presents himself to the trainer as a typical prospective job applicant. The trainer, playing the role of personnel manager, then proceeds to pick apart the applicant's story, as well as the application form. In this way, the student gains firsthand experience in what he might expect to encounter in the job market.

The first half of the fifth day is devoted to winding up the training school, in the form of a critique and group discussion on the book *The Big Decision* and any remaining general investigation cases that must be critiqued with trainers. All students are then given a final examination in order to determine just how much of the material they have been able to absorb during the week. The results of this final examination have always been made available to the students' employers for future guidance. The students are free to contact any of the instructors at any time in the future should problems arise where they feel they need advice and counsel.

Experience has shown that this formalized training pays off for the company in increased safety for the agent, increased chance of winning criminal prosecutions and labor arbitrations, and increased professionalism in the security department. For the agent, we have found that those who do well at the school usually turn out to be very productive agents, while those who do poorly have generally not been successful after returning to their companies.

We have found that most college graduates who embarked on this training are willing to do undercover work, especially if they can see that it will lead to a higher position in the not too distant future. Occasionally there has been a student who became so enthralled with his own ability at undercover work that he was content to remain in the position indefinitely. An outstanding agent, who really enjoys his work, can be worth more to his employer than even his immediate supervisor. Unfortunately, we have not been able to identify these unique persons in advance; only the true test of field undercover work can make that determination.

PAYROLL, OUTSIDE EARNINGS, AND EXPENSE REPORTS

One of the less dramatic aspects of the training, but one which can become quite important to the success of an assignment, is the handling of payroll funds, monies earned incidental to the investigation, and also incidental expenses. To ensure that the proper information on expenses is retained by the trainee indefinitely, a sample expense report is completed for a full week's period, including every conceivable entry that might come up in succeeding years. In any undercover case, the investigator must be allowed a nominal amount each month for entertainment, bar expenses, gambling expenses, and so on. This holds true not only with private security agencies but with any corporation and also with any law enforcement agency. Any of these types of entries on an expense report can conceivably be misinterpreted by accounting clerks who routinely process such documents and could even destroy the integrity of the undercover assignment if viewed by the wrong person. Therefore, each of these items should be given a prearranged code designation on expense reports for entry. In the case of company undercover men, trainees should also be instructed how to record payment of union dues and union initiation fees if it becomes necessary to join a union as part of the investigation. In this regard, it should be mentioned that trainees from either a private security agency or a company security department should be advised that the reporting of labor matters such as union meetings is against federal law and consequently should never appear in any written report.

In the matter of salary such as a semimonthly or monthly check, in many cases it will be possible to simply have the basic payroll or expense checks mailed to the home of the undercover agent. If the possibility of a mail watch is of concern, such as it might be with law enforcement agents, then a simple procedure would be to have the payroll department send the check directly to the agent's bank for deposit, and in this way it would not require his handling, and the funds would always be available. In the case of agents who are employed by private agencies, it is common practice for the agent to report to the central agency office in order to pick up his pay for a stated period. Depending

on the circumstances of his assignment, this could be an acceptable practice, but certainly police officers working in an undercover capacity should never be required to pick up their pay at
any official police station.

Furthermore, in the case of agents employed by a security
agency, it has always been the common practice in the industry
to simply have the agent keep whatever pay he receives at the
client's place of business. This is then supplemented by bringing
it up to a stated minimum and also by paying the agent on the
basis of each daily report. This same system is followed by a number of companies that use undercover men on their own staffs.

On the other hand, some corporations have found it to be
more desirable to pay the agent a stated salary from corporate
level headquarters. Any money received locally for pay is
usually returned directly to the corporate security department
and is used to defray the overall cost of the investigation.
Naturally, if the local money received is in the form of a payroll check, such check must be cashed, preferably at a location
common for check cashing with other employees. Under no
circumstances should the check ever be endorsed over to the
corporation itself.

Because of the tax problems that automatically arise in an
operation of this type, it becomes necessary to make someone
handling confidential payrolls privy to the undercover program.
It is this person who must scan the local payroll check stub for tax
withholdings before he is able to determine what withholding
should be made out of the corporate payroll check going to the
undercover agent. If this is not done, then invariably the corporation ends up paying more to the federal government for tax and
social security purposes than necessary, creating problems for the
agent himself in filing his annual income tax return.

This same procedure would hold true in the event that the
company undercover investigator found it necessary to work on
another company's payroll for a short time in order to facilitate
the building of a cover story and, of course, also in the case of
law enforcement agents who find it necessary to take outside
employment in order to maintain their cover story.

It is to be further noted that there exists a procedure with the
Social Security Administration, whereby an investigator can
change his name if it becomes necessary, but still retain the same

Social Security number so as not to lose any credits to his account. The form for declaring such a pseudonym or assumed name can easily be obtained from any Social Security Administration office. One final note of caution is in order for agents working on foreign (secondary) payrolls for purposes of the cover. It is necessary for them to pick up a copy of their own witholding statement upon termination of such cover employment in order to avoid entanglement for filing income tax. Normally, the addition of the withholding statements from all former employment, coupled with an adjusted withholding statement from the corporate level of the agent's employer should, if proper procedures have been set up, total out to the exact annual salary of the agent.

GAMBLING

For the new agent who has not had the benefit of formal training either in a police academy or in an academic setting, it is essential that any training program cover the area of handling of physical evidence obtained on gambling, drug, theft, and other violations. Common forms of gambling that plague American companies today are various versions of the numbers racket. In any numbers operation, the winning three-digit number is usually taken from parimutual figures obtained from the race tracks or from the financial pages of the local newspaper. In some instances, however, the winning number can be selected through a drawing, such as in policy operations which are common to Chicago or the bolita operations in the Latin American sections of the United States. Whatever the local gambling custom happens to be, the investigator should be thoroughly familiar with that operation and the method by which the collections are gathered. He should know how bets are recorded, payoffs made, and so forth. If he is familiar with the general mechanics of such a gambling operation, then it is possible for him to be more aware of how he can seize any physical evidence which may later tend to prove a gambling pattern. In the numbers racket, which is quite common in many industrial plants located in some of the eastern cities, one or more persons may control or operate it within a particular plant. The larger the plant, the more likelihood there is of more than one numbers operation.

It has been my experience to find some operators of numbers rackets in industrial plants to have an operation with a daily "take" of fifty to several hundred dollars. Considering that many number "plays" are nickel, dime, or quarter plays, the reader can appreciate the volume generated on any one day. In such an operation, it is not uncommon to find that the principal operator has enlisted the help of one or more fellow employees to act as "runners" in order that all bets and money can be taken. This, of course, necessitates that the operator or his runners make daily rounds of the various departments of the plant. Many of the bets are handled entirely by interdepartmental telephone. The agent should be aware of any particular employee spending a great deal of his time receiving telephone calls during the morning working hours. Generally, in most eastern cities, numbers bets must be recorded by approximately 1:00 P.M., and therefore, the bets are usually phoned into a central bank during the noon hour. In the case of horse race bets, there is no deadline on betting save that which is set for any particular racetrack.

The investigator should be aware of the possibility of encountering other forms of gambling within the plant, such as U.S. Treasury Balance pools, athletic event pools, syndicated gambling cards on baseball and football games, and of course crap games and card games. Most of these are definitely in the minority, or at least are not operated on a daily basis as are numbers or horse betting.

In a large numbers operation the operator frequently will transfer the recorded bets picked up by his runners to one master sheet of paper, which he will then carry on his person until he has the opportunity to phone in the bets for permanent recording. If the undercover investigator is aware of this, he can often find the discarded slips of the runners in the refuse container in the men's room, in trash containers in the factory, and so on.

Once the undercover agent becomes aware of who is involved in the gambling operation, it is usually an easy matter to eventually come up with some form of physical evidence. The slips should be placed in envelopes and the envelopes noted as to time, date, place of discovery, contents within the envelope, and of course the undercover agent's identification number.

Several actual cases of gambling violations which were handled by undercover agents are presented:

Case 1. Skokie, Illinois: After a number of months of undercover activity, the agent became aware of one particular fellow who seemed to have a corner on all of the policy bets within the plant (a form of numbers rackets). Regularly, the agent would notice that the other employee was away from his work station during several hours and would be seen visiting other employees in other sections of the building. Also, at break time it was frequently noted that coins and slips of paper would be passed to this particular employee in both the lunch room and the men's rest room. Knowing this, the agent set out to become friendly with the suspect and facilitated this by simply placing regular policy bets with him. Eventually, while leaving the plant together one day in the suspect's car, the agent was pleasantly surprised to discover that the suspect drove several blocks to a public telephone which he could operate from the seat of his automobile. The subject would then telephone in a long series of policy bets which he had recorded on a slip of paper. After telephoning, he would simply crumple the paper in his hand and throw it out the window and the two would then drive back to the plant. It was quickly established as routine for the retrieval of such slips to take place from the public telephone area by other security agents. Eventually the operator of the policy racket became so "flip" about his actions that he would pass the paper with the recorded policy bets across the front seat of the car to the undercover agent and would instruct him to throw it out of the agent's window. It was a simple matter at that point for the agent to fake the throw and simply palm the crumpled slip, which was then preserved for evidence. Eventually an apprehension was arranged at the time of the telephoning; and also information as to the exact location of the policy wheel was turned over to appropriate members of the Chicago police department, who were able to raid that location.

In my experience, operators of gambling operations within an industrial plant are seldom found to bankroll the operation themselves. Occasionally, a small-time numbers operator may accept bets on what are known as "lead numbers" of the three-digit series and bankroll these bets because generally they are low bets and carry very low payoff rates such as 4 to 1 or 8 to 1. Occasionally, however, the operator of a syndicated numbers racket within a plant may also operate his own independent numbers operation with a lower payoff rate with the actual bank being maintained on company premises. On several occasions, security officers, when breaking up a gambling operation, have raided and seized numbers banks on the premises which totaled several hundred dollars. This, in reality, is more of a pool operation with probably a small cut going to the operator of the in-house numbers racket. Theoretically, athletic pools arranged within employee groups are supposedly free of any profit taking by the operator, but in reality, it is quite common to find that the athletic pools are often rigged to give the operator a better chance than the other players in the pool.

Case 2. Bridgeport, Connecticut: The undercover agent became aware of the shipping clerk in a large manufacturing plant who obviously was taking telephone bets on the numbers from other employees in the plant during the morning hours. On several occasions, the undercover operative was able to answer the telephone on these calls and in this way was able to get a good "feel" as to the extent of the action. Regularly, the shipping clerk took his action from the plant to a nearby tavern where he used a public telephone to call in the bets. It was not possible for the undercover agent to get close enough in this tavern to the telephone booth to determine to what place the call was being made. However, it soon became apparent that the shipping clerk was also taking horse race bets which he would telephone in from his shipping office in the plant during the early hours of the afternoon. By arranging to walk into the office on a number of occasions over several weeks, and at the appropriate time, the undercover agent was finally able to piece together the exact number which was being dialed by the shipping clerk in passing on the desired horse race bets. A quick check of the telephone number revealed it to be the shipping clerk's own home. Ultimately it was determined that the house was being used as a central banking point for a gambling syndicate in Fairfield County. This information was then passed on to the intelligence division of the Internal Revenue Service for their follow-up and appropriate action. Later the shipping clerk was apprehended one day at noon time as he crossed the company parking lot enroute to the nearby tavern. On his person was approximately $187 in bills and coins along with the slip showing the total numbers action by the other plant employees for that date (Figure 3.1–3.5).

DRUGS

In recent years, the problem of narcotics and dangerous drug use has hit virtually all companies in the United States to one

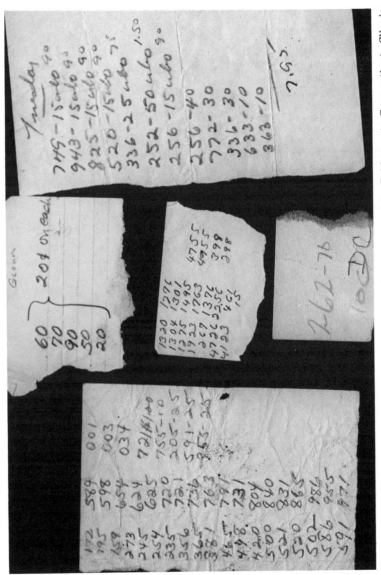

Figure 3–1. Numbers slips recovered by an undercover agent in Bridgeport, Connecticut. Slip in upper center shows plays on "lead" numbers.

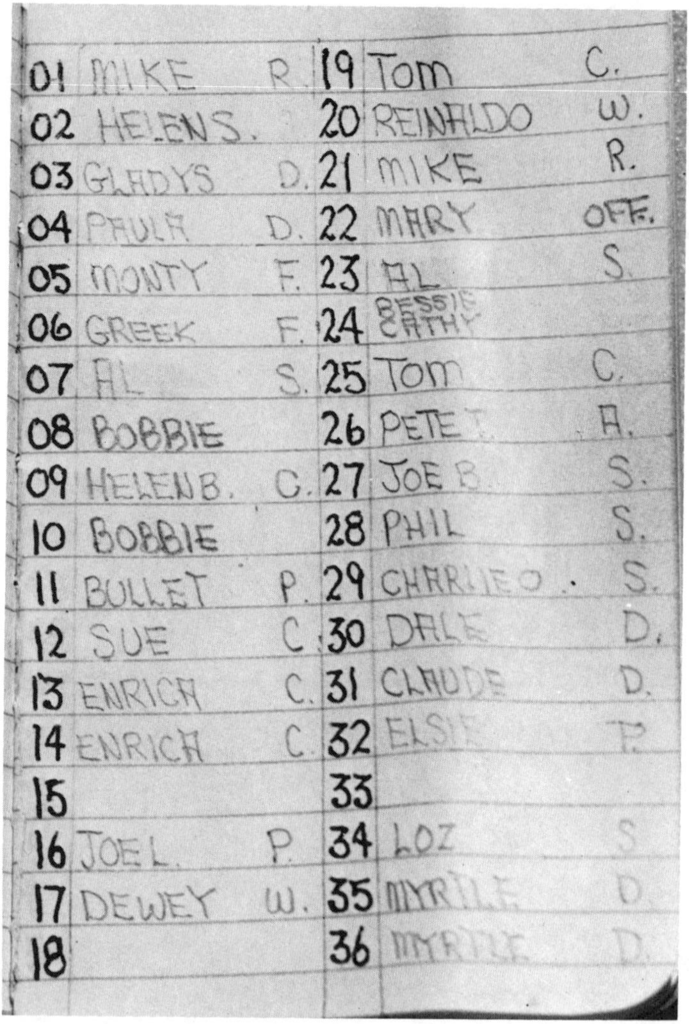

01	MIKE	R.	19	Tom	C.
02	HELEN S.		20	REINALDO	W.
03	GLADYS	D.	21	MIKE	R.
04	PAULA	D.	22	MARY	OFF.
05	MONTY	F.	23	AL	S.
06	GREEK	F.	24	BESSIE CATHY	
07	AL	S.	25	Tom	C.
08	BOBBIE		26	PETE T.	A.
09	HELEN B.	C.	27	JOE B.	S.
10	BOBBIE		28	PHIL	S.
11	BULLET	P.	29	CHARLIE O.	S.
12	SUE	C.	30	DALE	D.
13	ENRICA	C.	31	CLAUDE	D.
14	ENRICA	C.	32	ELSIE	P.
15			33		
16	JOEL	P.	34	LOZ	S.
17	DEWEY	W.	35	MYRTLE	D.
18			36	MYRTLE	D.

Figure 3-2. Gambling operator's master record of employee-players in a daily pool in Bridgeport, Connecticut, based on U.S. Treasury reports. Employees are assigned one or more two-digit numbers and are identified by first names and department letter. Booklet was seized during inspection of lockers prior to "bust." Its location was made known by an undercover agent.

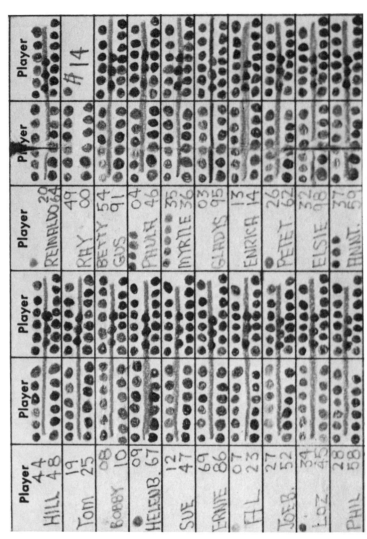

Figure 3-3. Addition record of U.S. Treasury Department pool in Bridgeport, Connecticut. Note that each player has two numbers. Dots in second and third columns represent individual "plays" for each number while dots in name column represent "hits."

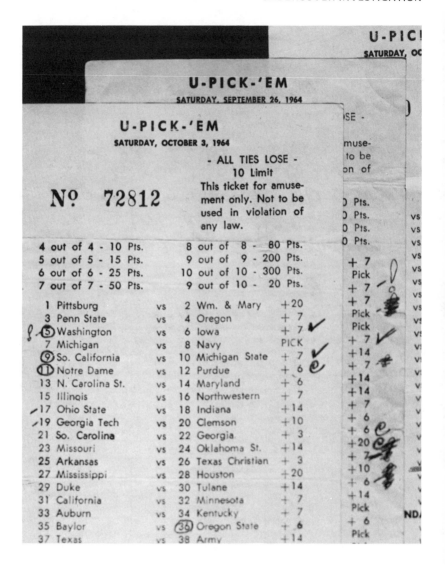

Figure 3-4. Syndicated football cards recovered by an agent. Selections are twenty-five cents each with a minimum of four games. The lowest possible payoff would be ten dollars. A printed admonishment against gambling is merely a thinly veiled cover against possible arrest. (Photograph shows top half of cards.)

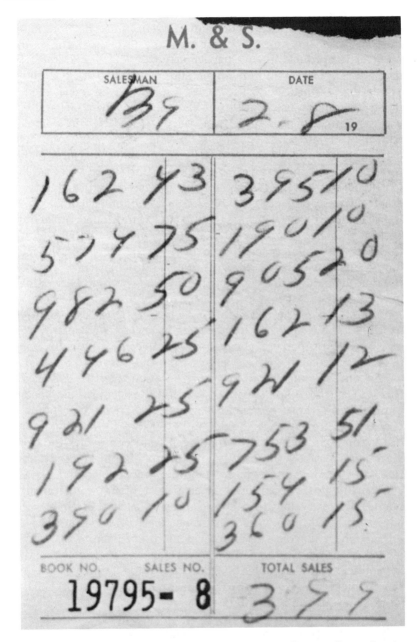

Figure 3-5. Numbers action in Northumberland County, Pennsylvania, disguised as a sales slip. Plays range from ten cents to seventy-five cents. Seized in an unannounced locker inspection.

degree or another. The undercover agent must be completely familiar with the current jargon or slang term used for various illicit drug products in that particular locale. He should know the drugs when he encounters them and be able to make "buys," preserving a portion of the drugs for future evidence such as illustrated in the preservation of gambling evidence. Generally, it will be found that many drugs are dispensed within company confines in glassene envelopes, plastic bags, etc. Marijuana cigarettes or "joints" are frequently found contained in a regular legitimate cigarette package, sometimes of the flip top box variety. Marijuana cigarettes are occasionally disguised by utilizing legitimate cigarette papers and filters. This is accomplished simply by removing the tobacco from a filter tip cigarette and replacing it with marijuana. The only obvious difference is that the end of the cigarette paper is twisted to prevent the escape of the marijuana. But when placed filtertip up in a normal cigarette package, it would be hard to discern that the cigarettes were in fact "sticks" or "reefers."

It has been my experience that wherever large-scale gambling or illicit traffic in drugs is prevalent in an industrial plant, theft of company property is always present. Because of the difference in slang expression or drug jargon from one locale to another, it would not be practical to attempt to define the various terms in this text and it should suffice to say that the agent should become familiar with those expressions in use. From the standpoint of probability, however, it should be noted that the more common drugs found in industrial plants and private companies today are marijuana, hashish (hash), and methamphetamine (speed). As a rule, the harder drugs such as heroin, morphine, and cocaine are usually not encountered in any great quantity in industrial plants. The very nature of these drugs is such that they would adversely affect the work performance of most workers to the extent where it would become evident to even the most inexperienced observer. On the contrary, workers who use drugs generally lean toward the stimulants from the amphetamine family, or the hallucinogens such as marijuana or hashish. Use of LSD by workers on the job is rare indeed.

Through the courtesy of the Drug Enforcement Administration (DEA), we present a glossary of slang terms for drugs. Many of these terms are commonly heard in the private employment sector:

Amphetamines	Beans, bennies, black beauties, black mollies, copilots, crank, crossroads, crystal, dexies, double cross, meth, minibennies, pep pills, speed, rosas, roses, thrusters, truck drivers, uppers, wake-ups, whites
Barbiturates	Barbs, blockbusters, bluebirds, blue devils, blues, christmas trees, downers, green dragons, Mexican reds, nebbies, nimbies, pajaro rojo, pink ladies, pinks, rainbows, red and blues, redbirds, red devils, reds, sleeping pills, stumblers, yellow jackets, yellows.
Cocaine	Blow, C, coca, coke, flake, girl, heaven, dust, lady, mujer, nose candy, paradise, perico, polvo blanco, rock, snow, white
Hashish	Goma de mota, hash, soles
Heroin	Big H, boy, brown, brown sugar, caballo, chiva, crap, estuffa, H, heroina, hombre, horse, junk, Mexican mud, polvo, scag, smack, stuff, thing
LSD	Acid, blotter acid, California sunshine, haze, microdots, paper acid, purple haze, sunshine, wedges, window panes
Marihuana	Acapulco gold, cannabis, Colombian, ganga, grass, griffa, hemp, herb, J, jay, joint, Mary Jane, mota, mutah, Panama red, pot, reefer, sativa, smoke, stick, tea, weed, yerba
Peyote	Buttons, cactus, mesc, mescal, mescal buttons
Methaqualone	Quaalude, quads, quas, soapers, sopes, sopor
Morphine	Cube, first line, goma, morf, morfina, morpho, morphy, mud
Phencyclidine	Angel dust, crystal, cyclone, hog, PCP, peace pill, rocket fuel, supergrass, tic tac

If drugs are present in the industrial setting, then the undercover agent's prime objective should be to gather evidence of such traffic and use. Normally, this will be done by making buys. Usually, the agent should find no difficulty in making a buy of a joint of marijuana or some capsules of speed. Naturally, any drugs so purchased should be preserved for evidence and later use in an interrogation procedure. The biggest problem encountered by undercover agents today will be in socializing with suspected employees who may regularly use marijuana or hash at social gatherings. A number of agents claim that they can simulate taking a "drag" on a joint as it is passed around in a social gathering. Many of these same agents also claim that they can feign euphoria or simulate heightened physical activity as a result of taking a "hit" of speed.

The whole problem in any of these activities is the fact that once the agent is exposed to cross-examination on the witness stand, his prior activities in drug use are almost always brought to life in an accusatory way and in an effort to either impeach or discredit his prior testimony given on direct examination. Agents who make good witnesses are often able to convince arbitrators or judges that they, in fact, did not partake in drugs and only simulated such. On the other hand, I have encountered a number of successful agents who have never had any prior experience with drugs, including marijuana, and were successfully able to infiltrate social groups even without using or feigning the use of drugs.

No professional security administrator would ever wish any of his security agents to become drug users, nor would he want to see their testimony on the witness stand impeached or discredited. On the other hand, the agent himself is faced with the task of infiltrating employee groups who see absolutely nothing wrong with the social use of the softer type drugs. Without question, this presents a very delicate issue for the security administrator in formulating a policy.

MARKING EVIDENCE

Occasionally, in a theft situation, the undercover agent will have the opportunity to discover and mark caches of merchandise hidden in a plant awaiting removal. An ideal method of marking such property is with a fluorescent crayon, but even adequate markings can be placed upon such property with an ordinary ball point pen without compromising the investigation.

In any situation where the agent is able to mark for future evidence a cache of merchandise or other company property, his report for that date should reflect exactly what he was able to mark, the manner in which the property was marked, and where the distinguishing or identifying marks can ultimately be found on the property. By tying the marking of the evidence to his daily report, it is possible to have a completely tight presentation of physical evidence at a subsequent trial, arbitration, or other proceedings. Likewise, with the recovery of any physical evidence on gambling or drugs, all the details of such recovery and marking of evidence must be reported completely in the daily written report. In many theft situations, it is often possible to recover stolen property which has been marked by the undercover agent and this, in turn, can become the basis of a specific criminal complaint for larceny covering that particular theft. On other occasions, it is sometimes possible for an undercover agent, working with another investigator assigned to outside surveillance, to recover evidence of property which is, in fact, in the process of being stolen at the time. This is illustrated by the following case:

Case 3. Pittsburgh, Pennsylvania: After several weeks of effort, the undercover agent was eventually invited to join a group of employees who met regularly at a nearby tavern immediately after work. The agent became aware that on each evening the shop steward, who was a member of the drinking group, would enter the bar carrying a small brown paper bag that was rolled and shut at the top. Because of other observations and actions on the part of the shop steward which were noted previously, the undercover agent soon surmised that the bag contained stolen merchandise from the plant. Working with another security investigator who had been assigned to outside surveillance, the men arranged to substitute a bag of fruit which was exactly the same type of bag in size as the bag of illicit merchandise. While the undercover agent diverted the shop steward's attention at the bar, the second agent made the switch by picking up the bag containing the stolen merchandise and leaving the bag of fruit. Of course, the switch was discovered that same evening by the shop steward, but he only concluded that it had been an honest mistake made by another patron of the bar. In fact, he requested the bartender to be on the lookout for his particular bag of merchandise should it be returned by the other patron. Ultimately, this particular bag of stolen drug products became the basis for a specific criminal complaint of larceny which was filed against the shop steward (see Figure 3.6).

Figure 3-6. Another facet of Case 3 was "Operation Shopping Bag." Merchandise depicted here was systematically stolen by one employee in Pittsburgh, using a shopping bag stuffed with newspapers on the top.

4

Establishing the Cover

The most important factor in any successful operation, whether it be industrial undercover or a covert intelligence operation, is the establishment of a proper cover story. Deficiencies in training, the art of roping, knowledge of the laws of entrapment, and other factors can be overcome to some degree. However, if the operative is to be believed and the operation successful, the cover *must* hold up.

In an article on industrial undercover work appearing in the November 1961 issue of *Harper's Magazine*, writer Morton M. Hunt states: "To build and maintain a successful 'cover' story calls for planning and discipline; it takes some doing for a lad just out of Harvard Business School to act the part of restaurant busboy without spilling the beans. An operator must wear clothes appropriate to his station, perhaps live in a dreary furnished room, and spend evenings with his fellow employees at the bowling alley though he might prefer to be home listening to the 'Missa Solemnis.' "

If the investigator is native to the particular city, the problems involved are minimized and are certainly not of any great consequence. In the case of a multiunit corporation such as McKesson & Robbins, we had to deal with over 250 locations scattered from coast to coast and from the Mexican to the Canadian border.

This required a certain mobility on the part of the undercover operatives and had to be taken into account in our planning insofar as the establishment of covers were concerned. To facilitate the establishment of a proper cover story, the trainees were given blank application forms and told to attempt to establish what they felt would be a proper cover on the application. At the completion of this exercise, each one was reviewed individually with the instructor, who would proceed to point out the weaknesses and loopholes in what had been established on paper. Generally speaking, adjustment had to be made for age so that the investigator would appear to fit into the proper age range of most of the employees who were currently being hired. Another factor that had to be considered was education. A company requirement called for a minimum of a high school education and therefore the investigator was encouraged to eliminate any reference to a college. In order to account for the time spent in college, oftentimes, prior employment or time in the military service had to be expanded. In most instances, investigators were advised to obtain local employment on a foreign payroll upon arriving in the new city. They were generally encouraged to hold this employment for at least thirty days. This time would give them the opportunity to explore the city. This was done by taking advantage of the public transportation system, if any, where the investigator would spend his off-hours riding various bus or subway routes. The investigator was also encouraged to make use of his automobile in an effort to learn the major streets and sections of the city so that he would be able to move about with some degree of familiarity later in the investigation. Investigators were also advised to scan back issues of the local newspaper for a period of time that would conform to whatever their cover called for. Seldom if ever were the investigators instructed to attempt to pass themselves off as natives of the particular city. Rather they were to make it appear that they had been in town for some time. Consequently, a job of thirty days in a restaurant could easily be expanded to make it appear that the investigator had been there for three to four months. The matter of references and reference checking with former employers was always decided on an individual basis, based on the knowledge of employment practices at a particular location. The type of past employment shown would tend to be similar in nature to the job for which he was currently applying. Specifically, however, in the case of applicants for a position in a drug warehouse operation, no previous employment with another company unit or any competitor was ever shown. If experience in the drug field seemed desirable and the operative had had such experience, then it was an easy matter to show this experience under the heading of military service. Another subtlety which was practiced by the undercover man when applying for a job in a union plant was to answer the question of "wages expected" with the phrase "union scale." To the union member who would process such an application, such a statement would carry a message all its own. Finally, trainees were taught the three *musts* for any cover story:

1. The story should be simple.
2. The story must be believable.
3. The story should be as true to the operative's real life situation as possible. In this way it is more easily memorized.

Test scores to be obtained, if screening tests are utilized, are another factor that must be taken into consideration beforehand. The investigator should be given sufficient copies on which to practice. In every instance, we attempted to have the undercover operative hired on his own merit, and thus the question of the application and test scores became very important. Even in cases where an operative could not be hired on his own, the preliminary steps were such that at least the application and the initial interview were handled routinely.

Although I am not suggesting that the typical industrial or law enforcement undercover case should be set up with the "staging" and the usual "deep cover" present in most international espionage cases, sufficient cover must be set up and maintained in order for the investigation to succeed. The amount of cover necessary will depend on the circumstances of the case and, of course, budgetary and time limitations.

From my experiences, a typical undercover investigator will often find himself working on what is called a "foreign" or outside payroll for a period during which he is establishing his cover. This conceivably could be a job in a local restaurant, tavern, or hamburger stand. Frequently, a job like this might last from several weeks to several months. Here again, the local monies received should be handled as previously indicated. This one feature alone makes it economically more feasible to have an investigator set up a proper cover story in a strange city. Many private agencies simply do not give their operatives sufficient time to develop a good cover in a local city. It is not uncommon to hear of covers being established over a weekend, prior to applying for a job.

Before beginning his assignment the investigator must develop a good knowledge of the area. He must be familiar with the local bars, "joints," rackets, etc. He must also immediately develop a complete local identification. This would include a local driver's license, local plates for his automobile, etc.

What might seem an insignificant point is made for the benefit of the new or inexperienced industrial undercover operative. On a number of occasions, I have noted that new undercover men, while attempting to follow through with the rule of "dressing the part" have forgotten that in applying for a job they should be putting their best foot forward, so to speak. In other words, what might later be acceptable and proper dress for mixing with other workers can very easily be insufficient to make an impression on a local personnel manager and cause the operative not to be hired. In one case, the operative had observed the employees of a certain establishment on their noon-time break and developed an idea as to how he should dress. However, when applying for the job, he was not hired by the personnel manager because of his appearance. It mattered little that he was no worse in appearance than the present employees at the plant—a sufficient initial impression was not made in the personnel screening procedure.

CREDIT APPLICATIONS

The matter of how to establish a local credit rating may seem like a relatively minor point but, if not handled correctly, can prove to be the undoing of the undercover operative and his efforts. Despite proper coaching, occasionally a new undercover agent will reveal his identity to someone such as an automobile salesman. Regardless of promises to the contrary, the automobile credit department or the finance company will invariably call the local office of the company seeking to verify the employment of John Doe, company investigator. Needless to say, it only takes one telephone call of this type and the man must be pulled out and reassigned to another city. Because of this, the new operative is coached that his attempts to establish credit must be based solely on his salary as an ordinary working man, along with the actual time on the local job. This may be difficult, but there is simply no alternative unless major purchases on credit are made in another city where his true identity would not hamper the investigation.

New agents must be taught that they are leading two lives;

1. The life of a security agent as recognized by superiors in the corporate office, and
2. the life of a warehouse worker, truck driver, or whatever the undercover assignment may call for.

The agent must be instructed that, for credit purposes, these two lives must never cross—there should never be any connecting trail from one to the other. Therefore, if an agent intends to use his true identity and job status within his home community for credit purposes, he must never reveal his city of origin throughout his undercover travels. An agent whose home might be Montgomery, Alabama, should never make reference to that city while working undercover assignments in other parts of the country, especially if he applied for credit under his true identity in Montgomery.

To better understand the hazards involved in credit applications for the undercover agent, the agent should have some idea of just how the system works. At present, there are three major credit reporting agencies that pretty much blanket the United States. They are: T.R.W. Credit Data, Trans-Union, and Pinger System. In addition, there are many local and regional bureaus.

As an example of the mechanics of this system, a retailer in St. Louis, Missouri, could, through membership in two of the above three credit agencies which cover the city of St. Louis, inquire about a credit background of our hypothetical agent from Montgomery, Alabama. If neither of the St. Louis organizations covered Montgomery, then undoubtedly it would be covered by the third, and there is a system by which one major credit agency can obtain data from another. Otherwise, it is possible for the retail establishment in St. Louis to directly tap into the computer of its parent bureau which covers the Montgomery area. Having only a name, it is possible to make an identification. By adding a former address or even a Social Security number, the search is narrowed that much more. Therefore, if the security agent has purchased an automobile on credit in Montgomery, and for some reason the St. Louis retailer has become aware of the worker's (agent's) Montgomery background, then the cover is blown. This is the very reason why the agent must separate the two lives for credit purposes.

For the undercover director, there is one saving grace in all this. There is no central computer bank nationally that identifies people by name and Social Security number. It is imperative for anyone making inquiries, to be able to narrow down to one or two geographic areas. However, it must be remembered that although there are three national credit reporting agencies, supplemented by numerous local and regional bureaus of the same type, they all will cooperate with each other in exchange of information.

WOMEN

It should not be hard for the reader to visualize additional problems which might be encountered by a female operative attempting to operate on a nationwide basis. It is much more common for men to drift from city to city where initial acquaintances and friends are easily made in restaurants, bars, etc. For a woman who is a total stranger in a large city, it is slightly more difficult. Accordingly, it is normal for the staging to be given additional time for women than it would be for men. This is well illustrated in the following case:

Case 4. Cincinnati, Ohio: Upon arriving in the city, the female operative located an apartment within commuting distance of the downtown area through a real estate agency. After securing the apartment, a telephone, driver's license, etc., the female operative was able to secure employment as a cocktail waitress in a downtown bar which had the reputation of being frequented by many members of the local underworld. After employment in the bar for several months, the operative had become aware of every racket which prevailed in the city and also could identify most of the leading members of the local crime establishment. Realizing that employment as a cocktail waitress in this particular bar could very well work against her obtaining employment at the desired objective, the female operative then upgraded her cover by obtaining employment for a brief period of time as a sales clerk in a downtown store. From this second job, she was able to make the transition to her desired objective at a later date. However, the important point is that once established within her main assignment, the operative was able to use the many contacts as a cocktail waitress to further her acceptance by the less desirable employees encountered on her assignment. Many of the people involved in thefts from the company were acquainted with some of the same gangster elements which the female operative had come to know at the bar, and therefore she was readily accepted into the inner circle of thievery.

IT'S A SMALL WORLD

Many people feel that the largeness of a particular city enhances the factor of anonymity. Generally speaking this is true, but the following case certainly points up that, in reality, it is oftentimes "a small world":

Case 5. Memphis, Tennessee: A relatively inexperienced bachelor investigator was assigned to a case in this city. He had been in the city several weeks and had succeeded in accomplishing the normal preliminary steps in establishing a cover. The investigator had set up a post office box to which his first paycheck was directed. Upon receiving the paycheck he proceeded to one of the large banks in the city and attempted to cash the check with a female teller by using his corporate security identification card. (Normally, investigators should never carry an identification card on their person when acting in an undercover role.) It just so happened that the teller was the girlfriend of a junior executive who was employed at the location for the upcoming assignment. To reinforce the fact that she could not possibly forget the investigator, he made an additional mistake of attempting to make a date with the young lady. Naturally, the reader can well imagine the reception the investigator received approximately three weeks later when he applied for a job in connection with his assignment.

It would have made much more sense for the investigator to have first opened a checking account with the bank by utilizing a cash deposit and then later using bank-by-mail envelopes to deposit his payroll and expense checks. In this way his company checks would be mixed with thousands of others that are processed routinely by the bank's bookkeeping department. Never once do they actually receive individual scrutiny by any particular teller who would also have the opportunity to match up a face with a check.

MOVEMENT OF HOUSEHOLD GOODS

Everything that an undercover investigator does should be carefully thought out in advance as to whether or not it will jeopardize his cover. Another potential hazard in this regard is the movement of household goods and the necessary communication with nationwide moving companies.

Most moving companies are only too happy to deal directly with a big company on the movement of household goods of their employees. In order to eliminate the possibility or rather probability that a cover will be "blown" by a moving company, the investigator should follow these simple procedures:

1. He should always represent himself as being self-employed at the point of origin in dealing with the moving company.
2. Because of the rule that furniture will not be unloaded at the point of destination unless paid for or unless guaranteed by a company purchase order, sufficient cash should be advanced to the investigator to cover the unloading of the furniture and payment to the moving company.
3. Again, at the point of destination, the investigator must represent himself as being self-employed.

The following case illustrates this problem:

Case 6. Peoria, Illinois: The investigator had represented himself to the moving company at Minneapolis, which was the point of origin, as being self-employed. However, he had preceded his family to the destination point and in the interim his wife received a telephone call from the local agent of the nationwide moving company. One question was "Where can our driver contact your husband upon arrival of the furniture in Peoria?" At this point, the local agent was told the name of the company where the agent was to be employed in an undercover capacity. When the furniture arrived in Peoria, the above information was picked up by the local agent who promptly telephoned the company. Luckily for the investigation and the undercover agent himself, the call was received by the manager of the local plant who was privy to the undercover operation. It came at a time when the switchboard was closed down for lunch, his secretary was gone, and one of the trunk lines was connected directly to the manager's extension telephone! Had the call been received by anyone else, it obviously would have blown the cover and another agent would have had to be assigned to the case, thereby increasing the cost of the investigation tremendously.

STAGING

In his book *The Spymasters of Israel*, Stewart Steven (1980) described the staging of Eli Cohen, Israel's greatest spy in history. In order to prepare Cohen for eventual infiltartion into Syria, his controllers worked out a cover story to match Cohen's own background as closely as possible. The cover included the fact that he had been born in Beirut, Lebanon, of Syrian parentage. The family, purportedly, had emigrated to Alexandria and then had gone on to Buenos Aires. Steven reports that at the time of the staging there were more than half a million Arabs living in Buenos Aires alone, with a very large Syrian contingent. It was in this atmosphere that Cohen successfully completed his staging within a period of nine months of his arrival in Argentina. His next step was the penetration itself—Damascus.

When operating a nationwide undercover program, the security executive will occasionally run into prospective assignments which, because of their very nature, will tax his ingenuity in giving direction to his investigator. Such a case occurred in an undercover job in Jackson, Mississippi. Unfortunately, there were no southern investigators on the staff who were available for this assignment, and it fell to an investigator from one of the western states. Realizing that Jackson is not the type of city where people drift in and out from other parts of the United States extra attention was given to the proper staging of this investigator so that he would have a better chance of being accepted and being successful in Jackson. The steps taken in establishing a cover for this case are cited in the following example:

Case 7. Jackson, Mississippi: The investigator was first sent to New Orleans where he spent sufficient time in various parts of the city in order to have at least an acquaintance with the city. The "story" was that he had gone to New Orleans to explore the possibility of gaining an athletic scholarship at a local university. After being turned down, it was suggested by someone that he apply for the same type of scholarship at the local university in Jackson. From New Orleans, the subject moved to Jackson. At this point, he proceeded to set up the usual local cover by obtaining a Mississippi driver's license and Mississippi license plates. The investigator also spent many days at the public library reading back copies of the local Jackson newspaper so that he would have knowledge of events on a local level covering the last six months. From this point, subject obtained employment in a local drive-in restaurant where he worked for a number of months. Again, his story was that he had come to Jackson to apply for an athletic scholarship at the local university, only to be turned down because of scholastic deficiencies. Because of the fact that he was allegedly without funds, he obtained employment at the local drive-in, which he ultimately used as an employment reference and a base for obtaining work at his assigned location. Even though he obviously spoke with a western accent rather than a "southern drawl," his stories of attempted schooling in New Orleans and in Jackson itself were accepted and, ultimately, so was the investigator.

Participating in a lower-level or mundane type of job assignment is quite common for even government agents. According to former CIA agent Mike Ackerman (1976):

In the afternoon I was briefed on my cover story. I was to tell people that I had taken a civilian administrative job at the Department of Defense. I used the story for the first time on Saturday night's date, a girl I had known since graduate school. She was not impressed.

"After Dartmouth and Columbia and with your languages I thought you would have set your sights higher than that."

I attempted to appease her by saying that I had only taken the job on an interim basis and was, in fact, awaiting induction into the Air Force. I was going to be an Air Police officer. She looked at me as if I had gone bananas.

The truth was that since I hadn't fulfilled my military obligation, the Agency had arranged for me to participate in a special program it had set up with the Air Force. Under the terms of the program I would, upon enlistment, be sent to Officer Training School. Ninety days later, I would be assigned to an air base for about one year. After that, I would be transferred to the Washington area and detailed back to the Agency for the remainder of my obligation.

On May 10th I was sworn into the Air Force and put on a plane for Lackland Air Force Base, San Antonio, Texas. For ninety days I marched, made my bed, marched, got my hair cut every three days, marched, memorized chains of command, marched, ran obstacle courses, and marched. I frankly never understood the need for all that marching. For years I had labored under the impression that the Air Force flew.

The training took about twenty pounds off me and got rid of my graduate school slouch. I didn't realize how much I had been rearranged until I got my gold bars and went home on a short leave. I walked right by my mother at the airline gate, and she never gave me a second glance. True, it was the first time she saw me in uniform. But she was expecting that, and mothers are supposed to recognize you anyway.

I've always suspected that I was one of the very few Air Police officers with a Phi Beta Kappa key tucked away under his handcuffs. The Air Force had honored me by selection to its elite unit, the Strategic Air Command. I was assigned to a base in northern California, where my functions were both base police and security. That meant that I got to book drunks and also to baby-sit the H-Bomb-laden B-52's and Titan Missiles.

After I got the hand of being an Air Police officer, I interested myself in other aspects of military life. There was no Jewish chaplain on the base, so I got myself commissioned by the Board of the Chaplaincy to conduct services and counsel Jewish troops. Being both an Air Police officer and a part-time chaplain made for a couple of complications and some very good laughs.

Chaplains have the legal right of privileged communication with troops. They cannot reveal information given them in confidence at court martial proceedings. In my case, however, my Air Police responsibilities came first. I was legally bound to act upon any incriminating information I received. So I had to warn anybody I counseled that communications with me were not privileged. It always sounded like I was reading them their rights. As you might imagine, I wasn't called upon for much counseling.

I don't think the Base Chaplain, a kindly and good-humored Lutheran, will ever forget the sight of me conducting Friday evening services wearing a skull-cap, prayer shawl, and a Smith and Wesson .38 caliber Field Masterpiece. I know that I will never forget the time I lived out what must be a recurring nightmare for every clergyman. My congregation got up and ran out of the chapel right at the high point of my sermon. The red light, which was situated above and behind me, had suddenly started blinking its order to report to duty stations.

About eight months into my tour of duty we were inspected by a team from SAC Headquarters. One of the visiting colonels reviewed my personnel record and reached a startling conclusion. I was summoned to his office.

"Lieutenant, you have a Master's degree. You speak Russian and Spanish and Portugese. What the hell are you doing in the Air Police? You belong in Intelligence, and I'm going to get right on the phone to Washington and tell them just that."

I thanked him profusely but asked him not to interfere, explaining that I was quite happy in the Air Police, which after all, provided me with more of an opportunity than Intelligence would to command troops.

I really didn't want him mucking around with my assignment. I was expecting orders back to Washington and the CIA at any time.

I got a lecture on how I owed it to the Air Force and the country to exercise my full potential as an officer and how I ought to put personnal preferences last. He was still muttering something about complacency when he dismissed me. I don't think he ever made his phone call.

In April of 1964 I was reassigned to Washington. For the remainder of my three-year military obligation, I would only put on my uniform for cover reasons—or to take advantage of military discounts on air fares.

THE HIRING

Unlike the informal infiltration of a criminal gang, in industrial undercover work there is a certain initial formality—a barrier that must be surmounted and crossed successfully without jeopardizing the cover. For purposes of this text it would be impossible to list every conceivable obstacle that may be encountered by the director of an undercover investigation.

Such factors as lay-off conditions with provisions for seniority recall, departmental seniority, job bidding, union hiring halls, preferential leanings of the personnel interviewer, and IQ or aptitude tests all serve to test the ingenuity and imagination of the investigations director.

Any undercover investigation should be controlled so that its existence is maintained on a "need-to-know" basis. No exceptions to this rule should be permitted. Accordingly then, what role should a plant manager play in the hiring process? Can the agent gain employment on his own or can the plant manager be of assistance? Should the personnel manager be made privy in order to facilitate the hiring? Should another executive be taken into confidence in order to place the agent in the proper department and on the correct shift? These are typical questions that constantly arise and include the old management argument of the effect on executive morale when all members of the plant executive group are not made aware of the undercover project. Experience has shown that investigations are usually more successful if knowledge is limited to one top executive. Even he should not know the name of the agent unless on a need-to-know basis. If the agent can gain employment on his own, so much the better. If not, then it may be necessary to have the top executive make contact with the personnel manager even though it may mean passing over one or more other line executives in the chain of command.

As to assignment to department or shift, again it is much better to have the agent attempt this on his own even if it means an additional delay of weeks or months. In the meantime the agent is employed and strengthening his cover. It is to be noted that much valuable information can be gained by contacts with other employees during lunch and break periods. Also, after plant hours the agent's work may just be beginning in the neighborhood tavern across from the plant gates! Movement of the agent from department to department can be detrimental, especially if this is not a normal procedure for a new employee. The investigations director must resist this and is in a better position to control his investigation if only he knows the agent's identity.

Union hiring halls present a major obstacle, but even they can be circumvented if time permits and a long-range view is taken. In so doing, the agent, when arriving on the job, comes with impeccable credentials. He now has a cover that is virtually foolproof, one given to him by the dispatcher at the union hiring hall itself! It is not uncommon for union day laborers to attempt to win favor with dispatchers and thus receive choice assignments of a more permanent nature. The investigations director need only understand the psychology of such people in order to take advantage and allow his agent to gain placement.

5

The Assignment

INFILTRATION OF THE UNDERWORLD

Many police undercover investigations which attempted penetration of the underworld have met with failure simply because sufficient time was not set aside for a logical approach to the world of crime. Confirmed criminals, for the most part, do not become professionals overnight. In virtually all cases, the professional criminal starts his life of crime at a relatively early age. Through criminal associates and friends, his life of crime gradually broadens until contacts and alliances are developed to the point where the individual can be classified as a professional criminal.

The police undercover approach to the infiltration of a criminal gang must be built along similar lines. The actual infiltration of the gang must be made by first operating on and by penetrating the fringes of the world of crime. Beyond that point, the actual infiltration of a criminal gang can only be done through referrals or "references." The better the set of credentials carried by an undercover agent the more progress he will be able to make in his infiltration attempts. By the same token, the more sophisticated the criminal operation, such as an organized crime syndicate, the more demanding the references must be for the undercover agent.

In attempting to deal with the highest levels of an organized crime operation, many times the local police have to be content with using informants. To properly infiltrate the ruling councils of the nationally organized crime picture would require years of effort; the selection of proper ethnic types for undercover agents; and the assignment of such agents to the task at an early age. There is little doubt that such agents would be required to engage in serious criminal behavior for many years before reaching the upper echelons of organized crime.

Infiltration of the criminal gang is really not unlike some of the problems encountered by the successful businessman or politician—the more contacts one has, the broader the base; and the better the quality of the contacts the higher one may go.

The reader should keep in mind that the art of roping, which is discussed in Chapter 6, not only is important to the successful conclusion of the specific case itself, but also plays an important part in the development of contacts on the fringe of the underworld and the infiltration of the higher levels of the world of crime.

Infiltration of the underworld is infinitely more difficult than infiltration of the industrial case. The techniques are basically similar except that more effort, time, and planning must be devoted to police undercover infiltrations than to the typical private case encountered in the field of business and industry.

PREPARING FOR THE INDUSTRIAL CASE

A considerable portion of the training period of any undercover agent, whether it be for a police assignment or for an industrial case, must of necessity include ample instruction on the various aspects of the assignment and the infiltration of the suspect group. The necessary emphasis on these crucial factors is given during the training classes conducted as a part of the Cluett-Foremost joint training school.

All the investigators are expected to participate in drinking activities in which other employees engage. Illustrations were made to trainees as to the type of drinking that they were apt to encounter and how much they should participate. As an example, we would point out to the trainee that in one city in particular we found drinking habits to consist of "a shot and a beer" in tandem. Obviously in such a situation an undercover man should not order a highball. The trainee, of course, was told that it was permissible and even desirable to feign slight intoxication but warned that he was to be careful never to overindulge while in the company of suspects.

The very nature of industrial undercover work is such that the life of an undercover operative can become lonely, monotonous, and at times frustrating. Unlike his counterparts who work overt investigations, the undercover investigator must be completely undercover and must live almost entirely within the cover story which he develops. The professionally oriented criminal justice graduate is unable to receive the small but vitally important day-to-day recognitions which would otherwise be afforded by his friends, neighbors, relatives, and fellow workers. This tends to have a discouraging effect on not only the operative but also, for young married men, the wife. No longer are they able to cultivate friendships with people on their own intellectual level but rather they must associate on a day-to-day basis with ordinary working men and their families whose educational level in most cases would be high school graduates or less. For the young, college-trained investigator, this presents morale problems of which his supervisor must be aware and must be prepared to meet.

Another facet of the training is to indoctrinate the trainee with exactly what he should expect to obtain in the way of results on the job. Unlike "street" undercover work, the typical industrial plant or warehouse does have some type of security controls and therefore a minimum of "action." In many of our undercover cases over the years, far more action developed in collateral activities on the street than in the plant itself. The new trainee must be aware that in all probability he will not encounter any theft ring in the plant but that the most he can hope for is to observe or learn of individual acts of theft.

Common sense dictates that a new employee in his twenties will not be invited to join a theft ring comprised of workers in their thirties and forties, who may have worked for the company for ten or more years. The only reason such a situation would ever develop would be if the new worker had a position in the plant which became essential to the operation of the ring. It is the individual petty pilferage, however, of which the undercover operative can become aware, which provides the interrogation leverages needed to obtain admissions of guilt. These in turn lead to larger admissions of theft ring activity if, in fact, a ring exists.

In other words, the new trainee must be made to realize that if his efforts produce even one or two interrogation wedges on any one individual suspect, his job has been handled to satisfaction. Any additional information developed should be looked upon, by the investigator, as a bonus. This can be easily illustrated to the trainee by pointing out to him that just because, during the course of a six-month investigation, he has only seen one incident of theft on the part of a fellow worker he should not feel that the suspect is only "slightly involved" or "not such a bad guy." What must be pointed out is that the investigator does not have the opportunity to keep this particular fellow under surveillance for eight hours each day of the six-month period. The investigator should simply ask himself mentally, "I wonder what the fellow may have taken in all of the many days and hours during which I was not with him?"

These points on expectation of results and premature evaluation of apparently petty suspects are important not only to the agent, but also to the company executive who is receiving progress reports. In essence, the investigation supervisor must take the necessary time and effort to inculcate the proper outlook on the part of the company executives with whom he is communicating. Not to do so will only bring on misunderstandings, inevitably shorten the authorized time for the investigation, and may even result in major thieves being incorrectly evaluated and thus remaining on the payroll. The only reliable method for evaluating an employee's degree of dishonesty is interrogation, based on information developed by the undercover agent, followed by a signed statement which is then verified by polygraph examination. Experience has shown that to make value judgments of any other kind is being naive and foolhardy.

Motivation (or the lack of it) on the part of the agent should never be overlooked by the supervisor. It is almost always impossible to motivate the college-trained agent for a permanent life of undercover assignments. The best one can do is to keep stressing the essential role of undercover in the total security or law enforcement picture and of course emphasizing that good efforts at undercover will be rewarded later with more desirable assignments in other areas.

Among the non-college-trained men it is surprising to find a great number of agents who thoroughly enjoy their undercover assignments, are content in that capacity indefinitely, and, in fact, have no desire for other types of assignments.

THE INTRODUCTION

The initial referral that will launch the agent on his road to penetration of the criminal gang is of utmost importance. Smith (1944), in his book *Counterfeiting*, states that the agent must be introduced properly and under acceptable auspices to the criminals in whom he is interested. He must be OK'd. Smith also states that the introduction must have the complete confidence of the higher-ups, and that even so, criminals will still remain suspicious of the agent. It is necessary then that the agent be prepared to repel that suspicion.

Motto (1971) also gives extensive treatment to the introduction. From our own experience, a simple but classic example of how the introduction comes about is depicted in the following case history:

> *Case 6. Peoria, Illinois* (continued): The undercover agent had been employed in the job for several months and he had devoted his activities to gaining the confidence of his fellow employees. One day at quitting time he was approached by another employee whom he considered to be a logical suspect in the case. The other employee invited him to "stop off for a few beers" on the way home from work. Both men proceeded to a local tavern located in the warehouse district in the city, which was known to be frequented by various professional criminals in the community. It was evident immediately that the fellow employee was friendly with and well known to the bartender on duty. Initially, no introduction was made by the fellow employee except to simply state to the bartender "This is Harry." Eventually, when it became time to leave the tavern, the "real" introduction took place. The other employee called the bartender over to where the two men were sitting and stated "I want you to know that Harry is OK." With this one sentence, the introduction had been made! It was not so much what was said in itself, but it was sufficient to establish in the bartender's mind that he had no need to worry because of the agent's future presence in the tavern. In other words, various illegal acts which regularly took place in the tavern could continue without concern to the bartender even though the undercover agent would be present. The undercover operative began to frequent the tavern on

his off-hours and he became aware that it was the center for a number of illegal activities such as prostitution, gambling, narcotics and other crime. By using the bartender to vouch for him and also the fellow employee from the plant as a referral, the undercover agent began to become accepted, to a point, by the local criminal element. Without doubt, this acceptance of the undercover agent by the local criminals, at this time, was at arm's length at best. They would be willing to tolerate his presence during their discussions of their activities, but to welcome him into their ranks would necessitate some better "credentials" than what was already apparent.

THE TEST

Motto (1971) points out that occasionally an agent working in an undercover capacity will be used as a courier as part of "the test" imposed by the criminal gang. Motto is quick to point out, however, that if the agent accepts an assignment as a courier either as part of the test or at a later date he should make sure that the receivers are aware of what is being delivered. In order to further illustrate what might be expected by the agent in the way of a test, we draw further from the Peoria case history:

> Case 6. Peoria, Illinois (continued): One evening, the agent was invited to participate in a dice game in the back room of the tavern. He was asked to hang his jacket in a hallway and then proceeded to the back room where a craps game began. The agent was somewhat suspicious as to the motive behind the invitation and later became aware of the fact that both his coat and his automobile had been thoroughly searched while the game was in progress. Obviously, the end result of such a test would either be further acceptance of the agent by the gang or his probable liquidation. On another night in the tavern the agent was present when a fight developed and a man was killed. The attitude of the patrons was such that the police were not called for one-half hour nor was any help rendered to the fatally wounded man. Although it was contrary to anything he had ever been taught and believed in, the undercover operative had no alternative but to remain seated at the bar drinking until the bartender gave the sign that the police should be called. Following this incident, the operative was ultimately invited to join a highly organized local burglary gang. At this point, a high-level contact was made with the mayor's office and through him indirectly with the chief of police. The company undercover man was

given the green light to join the burglary gang and to participate in several burglaries while reporting same confidentially to the mayor's office. Ultimately, through his efforts, a trap was laid and sprung on the gang during the course of a burglary but on a night when the undercover man was not present. This came at the end of the investigation and at a time when he was in the process of being transferred to another city. It never became necessary for him to appear in court and testify.

In industrial undercover work, strangely enough, the test has been known to consist of nothing more than an invitation or a dare to steal and remove company property. Most industrial undercover agents would have no hesitancy meeting such a weak challenge. These rather amateur attempts at a test can be contrasted with the following far more grim situation:

Case 8. *Covington County, Alabama*: Because the agent had not been able to secure employment at the company to which he had been assigned for the investigation, a decision had been made to make contact with the thieves by another route of infiltration. The agent had obtained employment at a local taxicab company as a driver as he felt that this would put him in contact with the less desirable elements of the community and ultimately might provide him with an opportunity to make contact with the suspected dishonest employees of the local plant. Unfortunately, at about the time of his employment as a taxicab driver, there had been an attempted kidnapping of a local bank official's wife in connection with a proposed bank robbery attempt. The kidnapping and robbery did not come off as planned but did result in extensive FBI surveillance and heat on certain key members of the local underworld for a period of weeks. Unfortunately, the new taxicab driver became suspected as an FBI "plant." One night, the local triggerman for the gang which operated the taxicab company took the agent into a back alley and placed a gun against his head. The agent and his billfold were then thoroughly searched by a confederate but fortunately no incriminating identification was discovered. The only identification papers in the agent's wallet were those that reflected his background as a merchant seaman which had been part of his cover story. Following this incident, the agent was put to several other tests which consisted of transporting various amounts of illegal whiskey in his taxicab. Apparently, all tests were passed to satisfaction as the heat finally disappeared and the agent was once again accepted in good standing by his crooked associates at the taxicab company.

An undercover investigator should not be reluctant to initially pass up the first invitation to join in such criminal activity as experience has shown that this can be declined in such a way as to provide the opportunity to join at a later date. This gives the operative's superiors an opportunity to make a decision to permit the operative to join a criminal gang if there is some useful purpose to be served, either from a company standpoint or because of company relations with the community. Obviously, the safeguards required to protect the operative in such a situation must be even more stringent than would apply ordinarily. Each situation would have to be judged on its own merits as to who should be contacted to set up such an arrangement. There must be complete cooperation and trust between the law enforcement agency involved and the company security department. Otherwise, it could result in injury or death to the operative or irreversible damage to the case itself.

6

Roping

Of all the things that an undercover agent is asked to do, probably the best mark of his success in this field would be his ability to rope. Without the ability to rope, any other talents in this area are pretty much meaningless. Many readers are apt to confuse the art of roping with entrapment. Therefore, an effort will be made in this and the following chapter to present the reader with sufficient material so that a definite distinction can be made.

Possony (1966) has defined one form of roping by stating that "agents may pose as spies to gain the confidence of real spies and to learn about the members and aims of the enemy spy system." Obviously, the above definition would more closely describe the activity of an undercover agent engaged in espionage or counter-intelligence work.

Looking at roping from the standpoint of an undercover agent engaged in law enforcement activities, Smith (1944) makes the following points:

1. Undercover is a dangerous activity for the agent, and consequently he must be able to identify completely with the criminal.
2. The more unsavory the agent appears in character and background the better his chances of success in roping.
3. The agent must be a consummate actor—his life may well depend on his acting ability.

4. The agent must have the argot of local criminals, their manner-isms, their method of thinking, their mode of dress, and if possible the agent must physically resemble the type of criminal he is attempting to rope.
5. When the occasion demands, the agent must be prepared to be arrested with his suspect and if necessary to even do time with him in a penal institution.

An illustration of this last point is made in the following case history:

> *Case 9. Minneapolis, Minnesota*: At the time of the "bust" both the agent and one of the chief suspects had been apprehended by company security officers in the act of removing merchandise from a drug ware-house. Inasmuch as both parties had been apprehended while in posses-sion of contraband, the agent "confessed." Shortly thereafter so did the real suspect. Based on information that had been previously supplied by the agent, security officials were of the strong belief that a considerable amount of contraband had been concealed by the suspect at some unknown location. Even though confessing his guilt of the moment, the suspect would not acknowledge other thefts or the whereabouts of the additional merchandise. The suspect was arrested and charged with grand larceny and placed in the city jail awaiting arraignment. Shortly thereafter, the agent was also "arrested" and arrangements were made to incarcerate him in the same cell as the suspect. Previously, when establishing his cover, the agent had used the story that he was from the state of Michigan and that there were warrants out for his arrest. Based on this, it was easy for local jail officials and the agent to convince the suspect that he was being held on the more serious charge of being a fugitive and was simply awaiting the arrival of Michigan peace officers to effect his return to that state. During the next twenty-four hours, the two men confided in each other of many occurrences in their backgrounds and eventually the suspect revealed to the agent the location of an old garage in the city where the stolen merchandise was stored by the case-lot. With this information, it was a relatively easy matter to obtain a search warrant and make the recovery (Figure 6.1).

The art of roping, as taught in industrial undercover work, is based on the old adage: "It takes a thief to catch a thief." This does not imply that an undercover operative, newly assigned to a case, should plunge into a variety of theft activities. To do so

Figure 6-1. Merchandise recovery shown in "Operation Lunch Bucket." A container was used to remove contraband twice each day from the warehouse. The whole operation was exposed by an undercover investigator.

would turn away not only the honest employees but the hard-core thieves as well. The older thieves would simply view such a person as being extremely reckless and a possible danger to their own welfare. Experience has shown that undercover agents behaving in this way are given a wide berth and generally produce little or no results. There is little question but that the undercover operative must begin with more subtle activities.

The following example illustrates how the art of roping might be gently developed. A newly assigned agent is working on a production line along with a number of other workers. Let us assume that this is only the first or second day on the job when suddenly the operative notices a member of management entering the production floor. At this point, the operative could simply nudge his fellow worker and remark: "Watch it, here comes the boss." By this simple act, the operative has now established himself as being pro-fellow worker and antimanagement—the first step to be taken in the act of roping.

Another helpful approach to roping is the establishment of an apparent criminal background. For law enforcement agencies which feel that their criminal records files might be accessible to the underworld, it is a simple matter to "plant" fingerprints, mug shots, and an arrest record for an undercover agent. In so doing, however, the planted record should generally conform as to type of criminal activity of the undercover assignment itself. It may even be desirable to arrange "pickups" or apparent arrests on minor charges of the agent in order to establish him as a police character.

A number of successful industrial undercover agents have been known to use fake news clippings about previous arrests. A favored trick is to lose one's wallet, containing such a news clip, in the washroom or some other appropriate place. Human nature being what it is, the average worker will usually yield to curiosity. Not only is the fake identification of the agent established, but his criminal background as well. Other agents have occasionally "dropped" revealing documents such as civil summonses in a law suit, notices of foreclosure, repossession warnings, final demands for payment, or a parole or probation officer's business card. Imagination can easily bring forth similar gimmicks to assist in the roping.

Another example of roping can be cited from the following case. This is a technique which would be used after a certain length of time on the job where friendships of appropriate strength had been developed:

Case 9. Minneapolis, Minnesota (continued): One evening after quitting time, in a tavern near the plant the undercover operative encountered a fellow employee and one whom he considered to be a possible suspect in the theft activities. At this point in the investigation, the operative had no evidence against the suspect except that generated by that "sixth sense" which is peculiar to most successful undercover agents. After a certain period of drinking at the bar, the agent began to feign intoxication and after a suitable length of time, he confided in his fellow worker that he was a fugitive from a nearby state where he was wanted for a series of larcenies and burglaries. The operative of course swore the fellow employee to secrecy but in the process, went into some detail on one or two of the fictitious crimes which had been committed. With the assistance of the alcohol involved, the fellow employee felt obliged to attempt some bragging on his own and revealed to the investigator the fact that he had single-handedly committed two drugstore burglaries for which he had never been apprehended. He in turn also swore the operative to secrecy and stated that not even his wife had learned of his actions. Such a revelation must always be viewed with a certain amount of reservation, but in this particular case a check of police records indicated that burglaries of the two stores in question were on the books and also the fact that the burglaries were still "open." Eventually, the type of mutual trust which was developed over the session at the bar led to further revelations concerning theft of merchandise from the company. This, however, came a number of weeks later because the operative was not pushing for information and felt that it would all come in due time.

A third example would be the act of theft of merchandise itself. When initiating such actions, the operative must be extremely careful to observe two basic rules:

1. He should be careful not to appear as the most active thief in the plant but rather to be content to be no higher than third in rank.
2. Many acts of theft can be simulated by undercover operatives without actually removing the merchandise from the plant.

Initially, the operative will not know who the honest employees are versus the dishonest ones and he must ensure that he is not apprehended by management as a result of being turned in by an honest employee.

In the event that he is reported to management, the undercover operative will have learned that the other employee in question is not to be "trusted" and in all probability is not involved himself. It has been the experience of most directors of undercover programs that seldom indeed does a thief turn in another employee. This is not only against "the code" but it simply generates a lot of unnecessary heat on the thief himself.

Another of the many guidelines to follow is that the operative should usually not commit or even simulate a theft in front of only one employee. This generally proves to be a waste of time and effort on the part of the operative. The operative should ensure that any thefts which he commits or simulates are performed in the view of at least two employees. The whole idea is that the operative is attempting to establish his reputation with fellow workers as being dishonest, and when such an act is performed in front of two other employees, the operative can be positive that when he departs the scene his actions will become the subject of a conversation between the two others. Once two employees have discussed such action between themselves, there seems to be little hesitation for continuing the discussion with other employees who were not present. On the other hand the "code" is such that, generally speaking, if the act is committed in the view of only one employee, the chances are that the observer will say nothing to his fellow employees.

One of the most artful jobs of roping, combined with a proper cover story, and adequate staging was that performed by William J. Burns in a lynching investigation which had its beginnings September 14, 1897, in Versailles, Indiana, as portrayed in Burns's biography by Gene Caesar (1968). An excerpt from this book follows:[1]

---

[1] Reprinted from *Incredible Detective* with permission of Curtis Brown, Ltd. and Prentice-Hall, Inc.

Case W.J.B. Versailles, Indiana: A band of burglars had been terrorizing Ripley County—breaking into isolated farmhouses at night, torturing at least one elderly couple to learn where their valuables were, and committing "other heinous crimes," which meant they had molested some local women. Three suspects were captured—an elderly giant of a man named Lyle Levi, and two of his friends, Henry Schuter and William Jenkins. The Ripley County sherriff went after two more suspects, a pair of hoodlums named Andrews and Gordon, and was badly wounded in a gun battle with them. A group of armed citizens joined with deputies in running down the pair, while the sheriff lay wounded. The deputies who were guarding the jail blandly insisted afterward that they'd been helpless because their shotguns somehow had been unloaded that night, when men with handkerchiefs on their faces forced their way in, gunned down Levi, Schuter and Jenkins, then dragged out all five and strung them up.

Were any of the jail's prisoners spared? Burns wondered.

Just one, he was told, a boy named Kelly, who was now in the state reformatory. But no one had been able to learn anything from him. He had obviously been threatened and badly frightened, and it was quite possible that he had no useful information anyway. Burns turned to the young detective, Steve Connell, and told him his job would be to enter the reformatory as an inmate and find out if Kelly did know anything.

"I don't know if I can do it," Connell protested. "The reform school kids don't even shave yet."

"Then shave at night when no one's looking," Burns said.

Deputy Marshal Ed Smith was a tall, rawbone Missourian in his mid 50's. Burns decided that he should go into the farm-equipment business. From his private-detective days, Burns knew a Chicago manufacturer he was certain would do him the favor, at least temporarily, of establishing a new outlet in Ripley County. Farmers habitually liked to pass the time of day in machinery salesrooms, as well as in general stores. With no women around in the salesrooms, they talked more freely.

"A stranger opening a store in Versailles would create suspicion right now," he told Smith as they studied a map of the county.

"Suppose you set up in the next town to the north—Osgood. When you hear anything worth passing on, don't take chances on any Ripley County post office. Drive all the way over to North Vernon in the next county to mail your reports."

Now Burns began his own part in the strategy. Introducing himself as "W.J. Burton" at the Indianapolis office of the New York Life Insurance Company, he asked for a job as a salesman. He was curtly informed the firm had all the salesmen it needed, until he mentioned that he was willing to work the hinterlands on a commissions-only basis. Then a sales manager, who clearly regarded him as not yet bright, welcomed him heartily. So little insurance was being sold in the farm country that few salesmen were willing to waste time trying.

"What I would like to do first," Burns said, "is to learn the business as thoroughly as possible."

Not until he'd mastered every bit of information about life insurance the Indianapolis office had to offer did he go on the road. And even then he worked his way toward Versailles in slow stages, knocking on doors in one county while mailing his promotion literature to the next, polishing his role to perfection in safe territory and advertising himself well in advance. In dozens of general stores and taverns, in hundreds of farmhouse parlors, he played the part of a disillusioned traveling man who had grown sick of city life and hotels and restaurant meals and was longing for the earthy joys of rural and small-town existence. His reputation spread. If he was not always welcomed, he was always believed.

Using county directories for his mailing lists and saturating every area with pamphlets before he entered it, he took several weeks to reach Ripley County—where practically every citizen knew by then that W.J. Burton of New York Life Insurance was coming. However suspicious the residents of the lynching area might be, none of them could accuse this particular stranger of attempting to sneak in. Burns' first stop in the county was Osgood. There, to the delight of lounging onlookers, he promptly tried to peddle a policy to the town's new farm-machinery dealer—a tall, laconic fellow who irritably insisted he needed no insurance and rapidly lost patience. The eager salesman persisted until a door was slammed in his face, and even then he insisted he was not discouraged.

"I'll sell that old mossback yet," he swore. "I'll be back."

He did come back—several times—as he solicited every possible prospect in the Osgood area. When he would return to the store and find no customers around, he picked up what information Deputy Marshal Smith had been able to gather from the talk he'd overheard. Smith was certain that men from all over the county—Osgood, Napoleon and Milan as well as Versailles—had been in on the lynching, and he had a few prime suspects to suggest. He'd also heard that the gun used to kill Lyle Levi was a .44 caliber revolver that had been borrowed from the window of McCoy's General Store in Osgood, then returned to the window, where it was still being offered for sale. But he didn't know who had taken the pistol.

All the answers, if they were to be found at all, seemed to be waiting ahead in Versailles. And Burns hired a boy with a wagon and an old white horse to drive him on down a dusty road that ran between fields of grain stubble and cut corn. The only hotel in Versailles was an ancient two-story building of whitewashed bricks on Main Street, with a tavern and a dining room on the first floor and sleeping rooms on the second.

The hotel fronted on the courthouse square. Any newcomer stepping down from a wagon in that setting might have felt that the entire community was watching him from all sides. In the case of the alleged insurance salesman, this was more than just a feeling. When he went inside to register, he wasn't exactly welcomed.

"The town is right shy of strangers now," the hotel owner told him. "Might be best to move on."

Burns acted puzzled.

"Didn't you hear what happened here last month?" The man eyed him evenly.

Bill Burns shook his head.

"Well, some men were strung up, and if anybody ever deserved hanging, it was them. But there's been snoopers comin' around stirrin' up trouble ever since. So why don't you hire a rig over at the livery stable and get out of here fast?"

"I've already sent my firm's advertising to this area," Burns said. "I can't waste an entire mailing."

The hotel owner shrugged and gave him a room. From its window, Burns noticed that the white horse and wagon were still in front of the building, surrounded by a group of men who were obviously questioning the driver. But this was to be expected. Washing a thick layer of dust from his hair and face and brushing another from his suit, Burns went down to an evening meal.

He ate alone, and when he entered the tavern afterward, a hush came over the place. Hostile stares burned into him from every table. His attempts to make the sort of small talk he'd made everywhere else on his Indiana tour brought only muttered replies and turned heads.

Finally, a grizzled tobacco-chewing character walked over and sat down with him—a liveryman from the local stable and very probably, from what Ed Smith had overheard at Osgood, one of the lynch-mob leaders. Obviously delegated to question him, the man made little attempt at hiding his hard-eyed skepticism.

How much did an insurance salesman make a year? the liveryman wondered. How much on each policy? How many folks did he usually have to call on before he found one who would buy? How long had W.J. Burton been in the business?

Burns pretended to be delighted to find someone so interested in his work. He launched into a fact-and-figure-filled dissertation on insurance designed to dull the senses of any listener.

"You thinking of going into the business yourself?" he asked presently.

"Might be," the fellow allowed, tight-lipped above his tobacco-stained whiskers. "Might be doing just that."

Burns leaned closer. "Then why not list some likely prospects for me?" he suggested in a low, confidential voice. "If any of them buys a policy, you'll get a cut of the commission."

The man seemed taken aback by the notion. Muttering that he'd think it over, he got up and left.

Indiana nights had turned cold, but Burns left his window open when he went to bed. Shortly after midnight he was roused by soft but quarreling voices below.

"We can't take any chances," someone was arguing. "He was warned not to stop here."

"Anything more happens," another voice countered, "and they'll be calling out the militia or something."

Burns had a small pistol in his coat pocket. But at least some of the half-dozen or more men in the darkness below were probably also armed, and there was an entire hostile town to be awakened by any commotion. He could do little but listen, wait and hope. The muted debate went on and on, most of it in whispers he couldn't hear. At last the sound of footsteps faded down the sidewalk boards.

In the morning he began working Versailles much the same way he'd worked all the other towns, calling first on such prominent citizens as a lawyer, a banker and a real estate broker, none of whom wanted any insurance. When he returned to the hotel, he found that his room had been searched and his mail had been opened. But this too had been expected. The belongings he'd left at the hotel were strictly those of any insurance salesman, and his mail was solely from the Indianapolis office of New York Life.

He spent the next few days soliciting the merchants of the town. During that time, he later discovered, there were inquiries about him with his insurance company. Moreover, some Versailles citizens evidently hired a real insurance salesman to check out Burns because another stranger showed up at the hotel one day. Introducing himself as being in the same business, he then spent the entire evening doing nothing but talking shop with Burns, vanishing in the morning without any attempt to sell a policy.

When Burns began calling on the outlying farmers of the area, he hired the very liveryman who had questioned him the first night to take him around. Outlining a route west of Versailles, he mentioned that he wanted to swing north to Osgood later in the day. "There's an old hardhead running a machinery store there," he explained, "and I'm going to write a policy on him if it's the last thing I do."

He found Deputy Marshal Smith alone that day, but Smith couldn't add anything new. On the way back to Versailles, Burns noticed that the driver seemed to have something on his mind. Several times, the scowling, bearded man turned and seemed on the verge of saying something, but each time, he turned back to stare ahead in sullen silence. The town was in sight before he finally spoke up.

"Did you really mean it about cutting me in on the commissions if I gave you some tips?"

For the rest of Burns' stay in Ripley County, the liveryman had a steady stream of suggestions to offer—most of which were still in alphabetical order, having been copied directly from the county directory. And Bill Burns could sense Versailles slowly relaxing around him. He no longer caused a hush when he entered the tavern in the evening. By the end of his first week at the hotel, he was being invited to eat with the owner and his family. Then he even began to hear fragments of talk about the lynching.

He showed as much curiosity as he estimated any insurance salesman would show, no more and no less. Gradually, he learned how the Ripley County sheriff, although still stiff from his wound, had actually been back on his feet by the night of the lynching but had obligingly stayed in bed during the festivities. He learned how the five deputies assigned to guard the jail had indeed found their shotguns unloaded, having unloaded them themselves. At the end of about two weeks, Bill Burns had been accepted to such an extent that, when he mentioned he intended cutting a piece of bark from the hanging tree at Gordon's Leap, he was offered other souvenirs: one of the ropes used in the lynching and a handkerchief that had served as a mask.

When he finally said he had to leave—protesting, truthfully enough, that he hadn't sold enough insurance to justify a small fraction of the time he'd spent in the town—the new friends this genial fellow had made were genuinely sorry to see him go. At about the same time, a Chicago farm-machinery manufacturer decided to discontinue a recently-established Osgood outlet. And at the state reformatory, an inmate who seemed older than the rest was suddenly released. Meeting at Indianapolis, Burns, Smith and Connell combined their findings into a detailed report that identified all of the ringleaders of the lynch mob, a good share of its members and even some of the onlookers.

Occasionally, an undercover agent finds himself in what could be called an "impossible" situation when attempting to engage in a roping activity. Imagination and inventiveness can often overcome what might otherwise seem an insurmountable obstacle to a successful undercover investigation. This is illustrated in the following case history:

Case 10. Long Island City, New York: The agent was given the assignment to penetrate a suspected group of thieves who were employed as
warehousemen by a wholesale liquor distributor. The preliminary
survey of the situation revealed that not only was the warehouse
organized by a labor union in a closed shop, but all new hires were
referred to the company by the local hiring hall which was operated
by the union. It also became evident at that time that this particular
union local was controlled by members of one of New York City's
organized crime families. Even the warehouse superintendent doubled
in brass as the shop steward. The waiting list at the hiring hall was
quite long and even the offer of a gratuity to the dispatcher could not
guarantee immediate placement in that particular location.

Using an entirely different tack, the agent and his superiors
approached the head of the local security agency which was furnishing
uniformed guard service to the warehouse. Normally, the tour of duty
ran from approximately 8 P.M. to 4 A.M., and the guard's chief responsibility was to prevent local neighborhood youths and others from
entering through the shipping doors and obtaining bottles of whisky
in a "grab and run" type of operation. Additionally, the guard was
to make a visual observation of the warehousemen as they departed
the premises as 4 A.M. with a physical inspection of any lunch boxes,
and so on. With the cooperation of the head of the security agency,
the undercover agent was assigned to the location as a uniformed
armed guard. As such he was someone representing law and order
and management's interest. The agent's task seemed formidable indeed.

The agent quickly established himself, in the eyes of the warehousemen, as a guard who was more interested in horse races and taking an
occasional drink than one who was interested in preventing theft.
Eventually, certain members of the warehouse group would offer the
agent a drink on the job. On other occasions, the agent would make
a point of informing the warehousemen that he would be forced to
conduct a thorough exit check at 4 A.M. because of an impending
visit from his supervisor. This routine soon fell into a pattern where
no exit checks were made unless an agency supervisor happened to
be present at the 4 A.M. quitting hour. Before long, the agent was
invited to participate in card or dice games which were held by the
warehousemen during their lunch and break periods, and he became
generally accepted by the group even though he was never taken into
full membership of their theft ring. Eventually, the case was broken
by virtue of the fact that certain key members of the warehouse crew
had given bottles of whiskey to the guard from the warehouse stocks
on various occasions. Of course these bottles were preserved as evidence
and were used as a useful interrogation wedge during the "bust."
Initial admissions, based on these free gifts of whiskey, ultimately led
to more complete confessions and full disclosures of the ring's activites.

In Chapter 9 a number of suggestions are made to overcome accusations that the agent is a company spy. Some of these suggestions are based on the premise that the best defense is a good offense. Occasionally, however, methods resorted to in order to overcome an accusation can have positive effects on the agent's roping activities of other employees.

The following case represents a rather bold approach on the part of the undercover agent that was fully discussed and considered by the agent's supervisor.

Case 11. Northumberland County, Pennsylvania: The agent was assigned to infiltrate a company operation that had traditionally hired only local people, well known to management. In this particular case, local management was not privy to the undercover investigation and therefore other means had to be devised to enable the agent to gain employment.

Although there was some initial wariness on the part of the rank-and-file union members in the facility, the agent gradually overcame this and started to develop some strong personal relationships with the various members of the workforce. All the time this was happening, the agent was aware that he was suspected by the facility manager who considered him to be a "company spy." Rather than taking a preferable management attitude on the subject, the manager used whatever influence he had to try to enhance this belief in the minds of other key people in the facility. Eventually, it became known to the agent that there was a certain amount of "heat" on him because of the allegations of the plant manager. After becoming a member of the union, it was decided to tackle the problem head on, and the agent filed a grievance with the shop steward against the plant manager for branding him constantly as an undercover agent! With the shop steward's support, a first-step grievance procedure was held with the manager at which time the agent pointblank accused him of creating problems for the agent by referring to him as a company spy or an undercover agent. The manager denied the allegation and the grievance procedure ended with nothing definitive being accomplished. However because of his direct attack on the manager, the agent suddenly found that most of the rank and file were drawn even closer to him than prior to the grievance procedure. From that point on, the manager generally kept his suspicions and beliefs to himself.

In conclusion, a word of caution should be expressed regarding industrial undercover investigations and roping in particular. If a corporation or security agency has its operatives do their roping by stealing company merchandise, adequate controls must be put into effect and adhered to. Without adequate controls, many corporate executives would rebel at the temptation placed before the undercover agent who otherwise might well become a confirmed thief himself.

An undercover agent engaged in taking company products or property as a part of a roping operation must keep an accurate log of all such items taken and then these items must be returned to his supervisor at the conclusion of a case. Occasionally, it may be desirable for an undercover agent to personally use such merchandise or in fact he may wish to retain some of the merchandise for personal use based on normal needs. If this is the case, then adequate arrangements should be made to pay for such items of company property as are not returned at the conclusion of the case. In my mind, there is only one method of keeping this system foolproof by maintaining a tight control over merchandise so removed—that is the administration of routine polygraph examinations to the undercover agents at the conclusion of each undercover assignment. This technique is used in a number of corporate undercover operations and is followed by many security agencies. I am unaware of any undercover agent ever going sour with this type of control in effect.

7

Entrapment and Testimony

As indicated in Chapter 6, the undercover agent must have a good grasp on the distinction between roping and entrapment. Not to be able to master this distinction leaves the agent particularly vulnerable during cross-examination in court, as the most common defense tactic in a case involving undercover work is to raise the question of entrapment. The reader should keep in mind, however, that entrapment is not a crime even though it may be considered immoral or unethical in its application. It is, however, a defense to a crime, and if it can be successfully established during a legal proceeding, it is a sufficient defense.

CONSENT

The general rule as to what constitutes a valid defense of entrapment to a charge of such crimes as larceny is well stated in the text of one of the foremost authorities in the field of criminal law (Anderson, 1957).

> In the case of those crimes into which enters as an essential element the violation of individual rights as persons, such as the offenses of larceny, burglary and robbery, the situation is somewhat different. Here, it

will be seen, the enactment must not be under such circumstances as will amount to the person affected consenting [permitting the act to take place]; or a necessary ingredient of guilt, the want of such consent, will be lacking, and the crime will not have been committed.

There is, however, considerable discussion by way of interpretation of the rule, much of which distinguishes between *active* and *passive* inducement to the taking of the goods. If an owner or his agent suggests the criminal design, actively urges and assists the accused in the taking of the goods, it seems to be generally held that such conduct by the owner or his agent would amount to a consent to the taking of the goods and the criminal quality of the act of taking would then be lacking. It is however, stated in legal texts that consent to the taking of the goods is not shown merely by proof that the owner or his agent remained passive and made no effort to prevent the taking of the goods by the accused. It would also appear to be no defense to the crime that the owner of the goods, or his agent, pretended to cooperate with the accused.

Case 12. Bronx, New York: During the interrogation of the prime suspect employed as a drug warehouseman, the suspect freely admitted that he had been supplying large amounts of pharmaceutical merchandise to a local druggist on a regular basis. The deliveries would be made approximately once each week and at that time the druggist would normally furnish the suspect with a list of requested pharmaceuticals for the next delivery date. The suspect revealed that on the particular date of his interrogation, he was due to deliver a supply of pharmaceuticals to the druggist at approximately five o'clock that afternoon. The suspect had already gathered together the requested merchandise and had placed it in a cache inside the warehouse near the dock doors. Investigation officers immediately notified local police and an elaborate plan was put into effect so that an appropriate raid could be made on the drugstore that afternoon. With the full permission of the security officers, the suspect retrieved the cache of merchandise at about 4:30 P.M. and proceeded to the drugstore. He was followed closely, and was observed entering the drugstore with the box of pharmaceuticals which he carried into the back room of the store at a signal from the proprietor. At this point, local police and company security officers burst into the store and placed the druggist under arrest. The druggist was charged with receiving stolen property. Ultimately, the case was thrown out of court on the grounds that goods had not been stolen inasmuch as it was not possible for the suspect to remove same

from the warehouse on that particular date without the full cooperation and consent of the company security officers. Consequently, if the
merchandise was not stolen then no crime had been committed.

Although most states seem to acknowledge the above rule, the
courts in the various jurisdictions of this country are not at all
uniform in the application of the rule to specific cases. It is therefore very difficult to set down any fixed standards for undercover
operatives to follow that would ensure that the defense of entrapment would not be brought into play. It should also be noted
that the majority view of the United States Supreme Court, as
first expressed in *Sorrells* and reaffirmed in *United States* v.
Russell, 1973, is that the essential elements of the defense of
entrapment is the defendant's predisposition to commit the crime.

INTENT

In cases where undercover men are trying to lay the basis for a
criminal prosecution, they would have to avoid originating the
crime or the criminal intent. For example, when the undercover
agent asks another employee to steal an article for him, a defense
of entrapment, if raised to a criminal charge based on such taking,
would probably be successful.

It might be more helpful to outline how far a private undercover man might go in specific cases, taking into consideration the
type of work that is usually required of him in an undercover
investigation. Although the final test of the activities of an undercover operative must be met in the courts of the particular state
in question, many lawyers feel that the general rule of entrapment
would permit the following conservative acts:

1. Assisting the suspect in theft of goods if such a theft is first
   suggested by the suspect and the agent's assistance requested
2. Giving the suspect opportunities to steal merchandise
3. Subtly suggesting knowledge of theft activities to have a
   suspect take the agent into his confidence
4. Inquiring for information about methods of stealing goods
   so that the agent may discover the modus operandi of a
   suspect and ascertain facts to catch him in the act of stealing

In addition to the above four examples there are probably a number of other cooperative activities that an operative may undertake to build a case against suspects in the act of stealing, so long as the theft itself does not originate with the agent.

There is one factor that private companies should keep in mind throughout when reviewing these guidelines—that is, they are all directed toward criminal prosecutions. A company should not in any way attempt to dissuade undercover men from breaking theft rings and uncovering dishonest employees even where the activities of the undercover operative might subsequently rule out a successful criminal prosecution of one or more persons. As you can well imagine, an operative might well ignore the foregoing guidelines and break a case, often leading to confessions and ascertainment of *other facts* which support the discharge of dishonest employees even where the rules of criminal evidence cannot be satisfied. Company security efforts should not be confined primarily to conform to criminal rules of evidence. If this was the case, companies could not realize the full value of a security force, particularly in the prevention of losses through the early discovery of activities by dishonest employees. The reader should also be aware that many aggressive law enforcement agencies do not seem to be too concerned with the rule of entrapment. Many of their most successful undercover investigations probably skirt very close to a technical violation of the general rule. Companies should always view, as their primary objective in any theft situation, the separation of the offender from the payroll. A secondary objective, and one which should remain secondary throughout, would be a successful prosecution.

As to federal rules on entrapment as they apply to private security agents, we present the following extract from *United States* v. *Maddox* in the language of the Fifth Circuit Court of Appeals.

Briefly, the facts are these. Suspecting theft as the reason for its inordinate inventory losses, shirt manufacturer Alatex, Inc., solicited the private investigative services of its parent corporation, Cluett-Peabody, Inc. to locate the culprits. Cluett-Peabody's private agents, making known their desire to "deal" in stolen shirts, were contacted by the defendants and arranged to "fence" the merchandise in Atlanta. The delivery of 300 stolen shirts to the security agents sufficiently fulfilled the conspiratorial overt act.

[1,2] (a) The defendants argue that the company's deep involvement in the conspiracy, to the extent of suggesting and arranging for the transportation, amounts to complicity and precludes their conviction because of entrapment as a matter of law. The argument overlooks the fact that private investigators, rather than governmental agents, participated in the arrangements. The entrapment defense does not extend to inducement by private citizens. United States v. Prieto-Olivas, 419 F.2d 149 (5th Cir. 1969); Pearson v. United States, 378 F.2d 555 (5th Cir. 1967). Moreover, the defendants received the benefit of the defense when the District Court submitted the issue of entrapment to the jury for factual determination. United States v. Groessel, 440 F.2d 602 (5th Cir. 1971). The jury found against the defendants. In any event, the conduct of the private investigators merely afforded opportunities and facilities for the commission of the offense, a continuing illegal enterprise, without initiating the criminal design in the defendants' minds. See United States v. Russell, 411 U.S. 423, 93 S.Ct. 1637, 36 L.Ed.2d 366 (1973).

In conclusion then, it would seem that a good rule of thumb for the agent to follow in avoiding the complications of entrapment would be to ensure that the idea of the crime originated in the mind of the suspect and that no actions or suggestions on the part of the agent caused the suspect to conceive of such criminal behavior. In criminal court, labor arbitrations, or any other formal proceedings, the typical defense attorney will use every means at his disposal to discredit the undercover agent and his testimony and attempt to either draw admissions of entrapment or at least create sufficient doubt in the minds of the judge or jury that entrapment was present. For this reason, several helpful pointers on witness stand technique are included in this chapter. The reader is directed, however, to Heffron (1955) for an exhaustive coverage of this area of courtroom testimony.

DIRECT TESTIMONY

The agent's appearance in the courtroom will differ somewhat from that which he used while conducting his investigation. However, the agent should not attempt to alter his appearance so drastically so as to be totally unlike the appearance of the defendant. He must keep in mind that his testimony will undoubtedly relate to his roping activities with the defendant and of course his winning of the defendant's confidence should seem plausible to a judge or jury: A radically altered appearance, at the time of the trial, would tend to work against this objective.

In most cases, direct testimony will be pretty much of a narrative type. The agent should attempt to give such testimony in a clear and concise manner. He should never attempt to embellish or even color testimony nor to betray any emotions of glee or disgust when describing the defendant's criminal activity. Many successful undercover agents have made it a standard practice to look toward the prosecutor or person asking the questions when the questions are of a type calling for very short answers. On the other hand, when asked to repeat in narrative form the intimate details of the undercover assignment and roping activities, many of these same agents turn slightly in the witness chair and face directly toward the jury when telling their story. Of course, in a trial without a jury, the same effect can be had by turning to the opposite direction and directing the story toward the judge or arbitrator.

CROSS-EXAMINATION

One of the problems with many undercover agents, security people, and law enforcement people is that they immediately become too defensive when testimony switches from friendly questions by the prosecutor to unfriendly cross-examination by the defense counsel. Some security people even seem slightly paranoid during a cross-examination in their attitude toward the defense counsel and his motives. It has been noted that many witnesses of this type appear to be so much on guard as to create the impression that they, along with the defendant, have something to hide. This, of course, is the worst possible impression that can be created. Police officers who testify regularly are not as prone to become defensive as private security agents who do not go to court regularly.

As stated earlier, the main thrust of most defense attorneys' efforts in a situation of this kind will be to attempt to show entrapment on the part of the agent. If no entrapment existed and if the agent wrote daily reports that were completely accurate as to that day's activity, he should have no problem withstanding an attack of this type by the defense. In other words, he has already told a narrative of the story on direct examination and the only requirement at this point is that he simply stick to the facts as previously stated. In attempting to show entrapment some defense attorneys will try to create a doubt in the witness's mind of the legality of his acts and, in so doing, prompt the agent to alter his previous testimony. This is usually accomplished by the defense counsel's assuming a posture of outward confidence that he has just discovered that the agent has done something of an illegal nature and is obviously unaware of the illegality of such an act. To the old pro, who usually knows more about that phase of criminal law then the defense attorney himself, this is no problem; but to the novice or rookie agent, this approach can be devastating.

Another favorite attack of the defense counsel is to attack the lack of education and professional training of the agent. Many defense attorneys will mistakenly proceed on the assumption that the undercover agent, in industrial investigations, is lacking in these areas. Here again, he will usually proceed on this tack by asking the witness if he is familiar with the term entrapment and what it means. Also, he then may go on to some of the more basic terms in criminal investigation work, such as corpus delicti, chain of possession, and so forth. The well-trained agent will have no problem with this type of an approach. In summary, the agent should always realize that he is not entirely alone during his ordeal under cross-examination. If need be, help is at hand on the part of the prosecutor in the case. To this end, the agent should make it a habit to pause or hesitate just slightly between the conclusion of the defense attorney's question and the giving of his answer. This will enable the prosecutor to raise an objection if he deems that such an objection is appropriate. Once an objection is raised, it may become completely unnecessary to answer the question, depending on the ruling of the court. By the same token, many prosecutors are reluctant to raise too many objections because it then begins to appear that the agent has something to hide. The prosecutor will occasionally allow a defense attorney to proceed slightly far afield because he realizes that the agent can adequately protect himself.

8

Supervision and Communications

MANAGEMENT COMMUNICATIONS

In both law enforcement and industrial security there is often a tendency for certain individuals who are privy to the investigation to make supplemental communication efforts with the undercover agent. This may take the form of a ranking police official or possibly even the commissioner of police who desires to have briefings by the agent and is not content to depend on normal communication channels. In the case of industrial security, oftentimes plant managers or owners of companies have been known to attempt to make direct contact with the undercover agents rather than waiting on written or verbal reports which normally would be furnished by the director of the investigation. All these approaches are highly dangerous and should be discouraged. Although someone of a higher rank must be taken into confidence in order to facilitate the undercover investigation, it should be made clear at the outset of the investigation that the agent will have only one contact (and possibly an alternate). No other contacts are necessary to review the progress of the case. Theories and other matters pertaining to the case must be properly developed before being presented correctly in a written report.

Occasionally, members of top management or clients who are privy to the investigation will feel that reporting by the agent should be more prompt. In actuality, aside from satisfying the curiosity of the management personnel involved, more frequent report writing generally serves no useful purpose. One of the biggest handicaps to a successful undercover investigation is the tendency for management to attempt to make corrections of deficient situations within the plant or even go so far as to take certain actions that will prevent additional thefts from taking place. This type of overreaction only serves to bring heat upon the agent and hampers his ability to develop a solid case against the suspects. It is clear that ground rules must be laid down at the beginning of any undercover investigation, that management must take no action of a corrective nature beyond that action which would be mandatory if a situation was suddenly thrust upon them. If anything, management should be educated to the fact that they had best ease off in disciplinary measures and corrective actions so as to give the agent more freedom of movement and more opportunity to build a case. The managers of undercover investigations for service agencies usually have more of a problem in this regard than a corporate or proprietary unit. A client can only be counseled and attempts made to educate him as to proper posture during an undercover investigation. In a corporate department, however, a director of security is usually in a position to simply cut off the flow of information to a designated executive should the executive start taking unilateral actions which hamper the investigation.

REPORT WRITING

In a number of private agencies, telephone contact is also used for a dual purpose, that of report writing. In other words, in those cases, the agent himself does not render a written report, but rather dictates his report via telephone to a stenographer or a tape recorder. It is later transcribed, edited, and prepared for client review. This procedure, of course, has its inherent weaknesses from a legal standpoint insomuch as the final report is really a "rewrite" job and often the raw data is not preserved as it should be. It does have the advantage, however, of helping the agent to maintain the security of his cover as there is a slight risk involved in the task of writing and mailing daily reports. Law enforcement agencies are generally divided on the method to use, and of course a lot depends on the nature of the undercover assignment, the availability of secretarial help for transcription and so on. Major corporations and companies using their own proprietary undercover staff almost always utilize written reports. In addition to the obvious legal advantages that accrue with handwritten daily reports, there is also the tendency to incorporate more detailed material than might be developed during a hurry-up type of phone call from a local phone booth somewhere. A good example of the advantages of detailed written reports is shown by the following case:

Case 13. Detroit: The agent had been assigned to a wholesale drug warehouse which had been experiencing heavy losses in prescription type drugs and pharmaceuticals. The agent had been successful after several months in pinpointing the local shop steward in the systematic removal of prescription type drugs each day. The quantity involved, however, did not begin to account for the inventory variances which the company had experienced at the last physical inventory. The agent, although faithful in reporting in detail each day in his written reports, was unable to make any further headway toward identifying other significant thievery. From time to time, the manager of the investigation would go back and review the daily written reports of the agent. In one of these reviews, he noticed that on a number of occasions, two or three female order pickers were observed removing empty boxes from the warehouse at quitting time. Apparently, the girls had obtained permission from the warehouse foreman for the personal use of these boxes and would remove them, three or four at a time, telescoped together. It became obvious that an undue amount of boxes were being removed by the same girls. On the theory that this practice might be the missing link in the case, the undercover agent was given the assignment to pursue a friendship with one of the suspect girls. Ultimately, the investigation developed that the girls were part of a highly organized five-girl theft ring operating within the warehouse. The girls were regularly stealing pharmaceuticals, almost on a daily basis, and were supplying various sources in the Detroit area with prescription drugs. The drugs were concealed between the boxes which were telescoped together and for which they had received official permission to remove from the building! (See Figure 8.1.)

Figure 8-1. Photograph from Case 13 depicts recovered merchandise being inventoried and inspected by security officers.

In the matter of report writing, most corporations having an in-house investigative department usually use a style of writing which is quite similar to the style and format utilized by most of the large service agencies. Normally, most reports are written in the third person and of course the undercover operative uses an identification number rather than his name. The reports can be mailed to a post office box in a preaddressed envelope with an innocuous return address. Reports should be written in such a manner that the agent does not spotlight himself should the reports inadvertently fall into the wrong hands. For example, in an industrial assignment the agent should not describe his first day's activity on the job by reporting all the instructions and job orientation which he receives from his foreman and fellow workers. A report of this type, falling into the wrong hands, could easily identify the agent as hiring records would indicate what new employee was hired for that particular depart-ment on the day in question. It would be much better for the agent to simply report the activities regarding himself as if he were sitting on the sidelines and observing the indoctrination of a new employee on that date. He can even refer to the new employee by his given name. Of course, he should not dwell extensively on the details of the indoctrination and job orientation, but simply report the incident of a new hire as a matter-of-fact routine. In a proprietary organization, the director or manager of the investigation can simply withhold the first of these reports from being reproduced and in this way the first report that is released will appear to have been written by someone who has been on the job for some time.

In the case of agency undercover agents, there is often the feeling that the client must be given something for his money. Consequently, when there is no theft activity the tendency is to fill the report with insignificant facts already known to management—petty violations, rumors, and innuendo. This type of reporting tends to wear pretty thin with most executives who have security responsibility. Rumors which are relevant should be reported as rumors.

Many beginners in an undercover training program will have had some background in report writing. Others may not have had sufficient training, and therefore time must be devoted to the basic structure of the written report. Police or security report writing is really quite comparable in many respects to journalism. Students must be taught to apply the five W's and H, as follows:

Who: The agent should describe the suspects or witnesses in the fullest. Many times, names will not be available initially, and the agent will have to resort to physical description, timeclock number, nickname, etc. Eventually, a full name, or identity, will be made known and then the agent must reference this in that day's daily report to refer back to the original report where the name was not available so that proper identification can be made.

What: The agent should describe as completely as possible what it is that took place on the job and what the incident consisted of in its entirety.

Where: The agent should describe the location of the incident, and if he is new on the job, he should attempt to give the description in connection with some references that can later be pinpointed to an exact location.

When: This pretty much speaks for itself, but in addition to day of the week, date, and year, the agent should also pinpoint the approximate time that the incident took place.

Why: In answering the why of an incident, the agent might very well be resorting to speculation, unless, of course, the suspect has given a reason for the act. When using speculation, the agent should fully identify it in the report as speculation and nothing more.

How: This is really the modus operandi of the operation, the means by which the suspect perpetrated the act. This might become very important, especially in litigation that takes place years after the incident. Without a sufficient explanation of the how of the incident, the agent may very well not remember two or three years later the method used in completing a certain criminal act.

For the further education and guidance of the student, a typical first-day undercover report is reproduced. It is to be noted that the report is written in the third person and in such a style so as not to reveal the true identity of the writer, who, in fact, is the new man on the job this date.

To: J. Kirk Barefoot
From: Operative #28
Re: Ajax Distribution Center—General Investigation

Fri. 3/26/82
A new man called Joe was apparently hired and started to work today in the distribution center. It was observed that he was brought onto the floor by the operations manager, Jack Smith, and was introduced to several of the employees and also the foreman, Jim Brady. After the operations manager departed, Brady was overheard to tell the new employee, Joe, that there were a lot of fringe benefits to be had by working in a distribution center as long as he kept out of the way of Jack Smith. The day was spent unloading a box-car which had been spotted during the night by the railroad, and almost no contact was possible with other employees; therefore nothing further to report this date.

Respectfully submitted
Operative #28

For the reader's further guidance and education, the following actual case report for one week's activity is reproduced. Only certain identifying names have been deleted, but in all other respects the report is completely authentic and is typical of what an undercover agent might be able to develop in an operation that has extremely loose security controls and resultant widespread theft.

To: J. Kirk Barefoot
From: Operative #15
Re: Manufacturing—General Investigation

Mon. Dec. 3, 1979
Nothing significant to report this date.

Tues. Dec. 4, 1979
Charlie _____ stole two heavy-duty extension cords from the shipping department today. He stole them by carrying them out in his lunch bucket when he quit for the day.

Wed. Dec. 5, 1979
Mark _____ quit work this morning. He got another job somewhere in Tarboro.

Operative talked to Mike _____ at lunch today. Mike said that the cutting table spreads were worth several thousand dollars, and that he would like to steal one if possible. He was talking to Willie from the piece goods department.

Melton _____ said he will definitely have enough shirts to move a load at Christmas, so operative is waiting for Melton to make his move.

Thurs. Dec. 6, 1979
Mule showed the operative today how to steal small items from the plant, by concealing them inside of pants legs. He said many employees steal by this method.

Charlie _____ stole a length of cloth today by carrying it out in his lunch bucket. He waited until 6:00 to carry it out. He usually doesn't conceal anything in his box until after 4:00, when most people have left for the day.

Fri. Dec. 7, 1979
The operative today saw Don _____ , one of the drivers, carry out a
DO-1 box which was given to him by Ben _____. The box was sealed
tight at both ends. As soon as Don got the box he deposited it in the
cab of his truck and reentered the plant. Because of the condition of
the box and Don's actions, the operative is sure the box contained
stolen clothing.

The B/M working in the piece goods department is Earl _____ a.k.a.
"Willie." The operative mistakenly identified him as Willie _____.
He is still looking to steal some small bolts of cloth. Dallas and Murphy
have stopped their loan business until after Christmas.

Sat. Dec. 8, 1979
No work today.

Respectfully submitted
Operative # 15

Any training program should contain sufficient examples and
illustrations to a new agent as to what reports should contain.
One of the byproducts of industrial undercover investigations is
collateral information made available to management which can
later be of help in strengthening operating procedures. In addition
to the more obvious breaches of security controls, many executives want violations of plant rules reported, along with examples
of poor or incompetent supervision, safety violations, bad house-
keeping, and similar troublesome areas. It is not unheard of for
highly intelligent and experienced agents to be able to put their
finger on production bottlenecks and even make major contribu-
tions to the overall quality control. This type of effort by the
agent has been known to stop losses, other than theft, which may
be running at tens of thousands of dollars per year. It is recognized
that in industrial undercover work there will be days when the
pressure of work alone precludes the agent developing any significant information. On such days, the agents should simply record
the date and simply state "Nothing significant to report this
date." To do otherwise is only a waste of the investigator's time
in trying to compose a meaningless report for the day and also
a waste of secretarial time in typing such a report. The investigator
should be instructed to simply make the entry described above

and not to mail the report until something useful has developed on the job. In other words, the required frequency of reporting should not be longer than one week, but in the event that something of significance can be reported, then the report can be mailed on a daily basis. This type of policy removes a great deal of unnecessary pressure from the undercover agent.

MULTIPLE AGENTS

A word of caution is in order for the undercover investigation supervisor. Earlier references have been made about the use of an outside agent, working "the street," coordinating with the undercover agent. This contact is obviously necessary. In the assignment of multiple inside agents, however, the supervisor should always operate on a need-to-know basis. Agent A should never be aware of the presence of Agent B on the job and vice versa. Setting aside any questions of loyalty, integrity, and judgment, it must be recognized that the exposure of an agent can easily result in threats or physical violence. Such threats or physical pressures could easily lead to a bargaining posture for the exposed agent who is privy to the existence of a second or third agent. Such an approach may require more editing of reports and direction given by the supervisor so that agents are not pursuing each other. Obviously though, the risk of multiple exposure is well worth the precautions taken.

9

The Burn

Probably one of the most critical times for any undercover operative is when he is either accused directly or indirectly by his fellow workers of being a "company spy," a "stool pigeon," a "rat fink," or some similar name. From the standpoint of the investigation itself, probably the worst occurrence would be to have the undercover operative suspected by his fellow employees but never accused. Without an accusation being made, the operative is never really aware of the suspicion and therefore cannot take the proper steps to overcome it.

In one case a newly assigned operative on his first case had spent approximately four to five months and developed virtually no information. Eventually, the case was broken through another lead and this in itself gave an opportunity to analyze what had gone wrong with the undercover phase of the investigation. Upon close analysis, based on statements made by the suspects under interrogation, it was learned that almost from the first day of his assignment on the job, the undercover operative asked an unusual amount of pointed questions about the operation of the plant and personalities involved. Within several days he was known to his fellow workers as the "eye spy" and never succeeded in becoming close to anyone with the exception of one individual who, being ostracized by the rest of the group, was not taken into their confidence. Without knowing that he was under suspicion, the agent simply was unproductive for the period of time involved. He never realized that anything had gone amiss.

There are a number of steps, however, that can be taken if the accusation is made either directly or indirectly to the operative. In every training class investigators must be lectured extensively on this. Examples in previous cases can be cited, showing where the investigator or even his superiors reacted in an adverse or correct fashion, whichever the case may be. Experience over the years has shown that there are three effective ways to overcome the heat generated by such suspicions on the part of fellow employees. Essentially, the investigators should be told to react in three ways:

1. The investigator should become "fighting mad" at such an allegation or even any innuendo in that direction. It should be stressed to the trainees that this is meant not only figuratively but literally if the occasion demands. In one particular case, an investigator was forced to take rather drastic measures in a secluded part of the warehouse one day with a particular individual who was attempting to portray him as a company spy. As a result of this encounter, the suspicion ceased and no more statements of this type were made.
2. A second effective way to overcome this type of hindrance is to use the same type of name calling and make the same accusations against the main perpetrator of the stories. For some reason this seems to throw the accuser off stride.
3. The third and probably the most effective of the three steps to be taken is to have the operative increase or step up his own personal stealing activities. It is possible to cite example after example where the first two steps were largely unproductive but an increase in theft activity seemed to confuse everyone and completely allay suspicions. Many a suspect has subsequently told our interrogators at the conclusion of the case that "I always thought that John Doe was a company detective until I put him to the test to determine if he would steal. When he did, then I became convinced that he was OK." Such reasoning, of course, is completely illogical, but nevertheless is the type of thinking which seems to make sense to the average thieving worker.

The supervisor of undercover activities should be aware that certain employees or groups of employees in some plants regularly make it a habit to accuse any new employee of being a company spy. The theory is that if the person reacts adversely and quits the job, then their point has been made. On the other hand, if he can withstand the pressure and overcome it, then perhaps he is not a spy. This situation is well illustrated in the continuation of a foregoing case:

Case 13. Detroit (continued): The agent had only been assigned to the drug warehouse for a period of approximately four weeks when he was suddenly accused by a fellow worker of being a company spy. On the following day, several other employees also made references along the same vein. Both the investigator and his supervisor were completely shocked as every precaution had been taken with local management to ensure the security of the operation. Although the agent hadn't been able to secure a job on his own, he had been hired without any undue attention and only the two top persons in local management knew of his existence. The only logical conclusion at the time was that there had been a leak in the case and because of concern for the agent's safety in the Detroit area he was quietly removed from the case and reassigned.

Several months went by before another attempt at infiltration of the work force was made, and at that time a second agent was able to secure employment on his own initiative and without any help or even knowledge of management. After approximately one month on the job, this second agent was suddenly accused one day by the same people who had accused the first agent of being a company spy. The agent reacted in accordance with his prior training by becoming indignant and accusing his accusers of being company spies. Shortly thereafter, a decision was made—inasmuch as there was no possibility of a management leak, that the agent would attempt to work his way out of the spotlight and ultimately into the confidence of his accusers. This was accomplished basically through a planned and steady program of roping in the form of theft of company merchandise. Ultimately, the employees confided in the agent that for a number of years it had been a common practice to accuse each new employee coming onto the job. This was a standard defensive tactic used by the company thieves and had probably been successful on a number of occasions. As indicated in the earlier case example, the agent went on to conclude a successful case involving a highly organized female theft ring.

In conclusion, every undercover agent should realize that unless he has made a blunder of some type or has not followed proper guidelines, the suspicions directed toward him by fellow workers or criminals are just that—suspicions. As long as the suspicions cannot be confirmed in an accuser's mind, it is possible in most cases for the agent to overcome suspicious attitudes and go on to conclude a successful investigation. Admittedly, this requires a lot of "cool" on the part of the agent, and many security and law enforcement personnel would not possess the ability to overcome such suspicions. But then not all security and law enforcement personnel have the inherent ability to do a good undercover investigation. Without question, undercover work demands its own *special* breed of person.

10

Shopping Investigations and Surveillance

One way the undercover handler can keep up the morale of the agents is to give them specialized assignments, interspersed with the undercover jobs. Normally, these assignments might very well take the form of shopping investigations or, perhaps, surveillance—either moving or stationary. In the belief that a new security agent should have at least some familiarization with either shopping or surveillance cases, this chapter presents an overview of both topics so that the rookie agent will not be completely inundated when first presented with such assignments. It is not the intention of this text to develop skills of shopping investigators or perfect the art of surveillance as this can only be done through actual street experience and on-the-job training.

SHOPPING INVESTIGATIONS[1]

A major form of street type undercover investigations used today is called "shopping." Shopping investigators are used primarily

---

[1] The remainder of the chapter is adapted from *Employee Theft Investigation* by J. Kirk Barefoot. Boston: Butterworth Publishers, 1979.

to service the retail store industry, but may also be utilized in other types of establishments such as restaurants, hotels, and bars. For purposes of illustration, however, we shall restrict our discussion to shopping investigations directed toward the retail store industry.

Shopping investigations are offered by a number of private agencies around the country who service the retail field. In recent years, a number of larger retail companies have undertaken shopping investigations on an in-house basis.

Service and Integrity Shopping

Basically, shopping investigations can be broken down into two types: service shopping and integrity shopping. The old rationale behind service and integrity shopping was that they provided management with a tool to evaluate the type of service being rendered by the salespeople to the customer (service shopping) as well as an honesty test of the personnel themselves (integrity shopping). Many security chiefs in recent years have come to question the advisability of combining the two types of shopping into one investigation. In increasing numbers, retail security managers have come to the conclusion that integrity shopping is compromised or weakened to some extent when it is combined with service shopping. The reason for this is that the investigator must give so much concentration to reporting aspects of service shopping that he is unable to devote sufficient attention to the techniques needed to ensure a good integrity shop. Furthermore, many members of shopping investigation teams are excellent at service shopping but are poor producers when it comes to making integrity shops.

Integrity Shopping Techniques

Essentially, an integrity shop can be defined as creating an atmosphere in which the sales clerk will be likely to commit a dishonest act if he has the propensity to do so. Here again, this is not to be confused with entrapment. Integrity shopping gives the thieving employee an opportunity to do the very thing he does several or more times a day with legitimate customers when the opportunity presents itself. The techniques used by shopping crews are many and varied in their approach, but all have in common the fact that identification of the questionable transaction can be made by so-called tie-down sales which are properly recorded on the cash register by other members of the shopping investigation team. A typical integrity shopping crew will consist of two or preferably three people. The best shopping crews seem to be made up of full-time shoppers who have developed their art and are very proficient at it. An alternative to a full-time shopping crew would be a nucleus of at least one full-time or lead shopper, supplemented by part-time shoppers. Often, part-time shoppers can be recruited from the ranks of homemakers who at one time or another have worked as a member of a full-time shopping crew.

The crew is usually directed by a so-called lead shopper or crew chief who is responsible for dispensing of the cash to make the purchases, transporting the team, and working out the routing and schedule. The crew chief will also act as liaison with his or her principal in the agency office or, in an in-house investigation, with the retail security manager.

It will normally be up to the agency supervisor or the retail security manager to make arrangements with the crew chief for the storage of the purchases while the particular series of stores are being shopped over a period of days. Ultimately, all merchandise is normally turned in to the company for full credit and this is usually handled through a high-ranking member of the controller's staff of the store. In this way, rank-and-file sales personnel are not aware of shopping investigation merchandise being returned for credit. Figures 10-1 and 10-2 are examples of some of the report forms used by either agency or in-house shopping investigators.

TAILING AND FOOT SURVEILLANCE

Moving and stationary surveillance capabilities are required skills for any well-rounded private security operation. Not only are surveillances often necessary to augment inside undercover operations, but often they may represent the only means of building a case against a suspect. Even in the case of street type undercover work where penetration of a certain location or the roping of a particular individual is indicated, surveillance is almost always a first step.

Date Feb 3-9, 1978 Unit	Opr.	Start	End	Out	Hours	Issue	Mdse.
Cashier MΔ	M.Δ.	600.⁰⁰			18	200.⁰⁰	189.⁹²
End Mi.	B.0.				13	200.⁰⁰	191.50
Begin Mi.	C.N.				18	200.⁰⁰	160.65
Total Mi.							
Car Used						600.⁰⁰	542.07

Store	M.Δ.	B.0.	C.N.	Entries	T	Total
Case #	4.65	12.99	8.75	26.39		
Feb. 3, 1978		3.25	16.89	14.14	6	6
Boyd's	18.25	21.79		40.04		
Clayton	22.90	38.03	19.64	80.57		80.57
Case #	19.95	8.29		28.24		
Feb. 4, 1978	16.75	28.76	16.84	62.35	5	11
Boyd's	13.99		22.50	36.49		
Crestwood	50.69	37.05	39.34	127.08		207.65
Case #	6.64		32.55	39.19		
Feb. 5, 1978	17.92		2.60	20.52	4	15
Boyd's	21.75			21.75		
Jamestown	46.31		35.15	81.46		289.11
Case #	17.95	36.06	16.22	70.23		
Feb. 7, 1978	18.92	19.99		38.91	6	21
Boyd's		15.50	19.75	35.25		
Northwest Plaza	36.87	71.55	35.97	144.39		433.50
Case #	8.75	16.95	2.45	28.15		
Feb. 8, 1978	3.50	27.92		31.42	5	26
Boyd's	13.85		16.99	30.84		
St. Clair	26.10	44.87	19.44	90.41		523.91

Figure 10-1. A Cash and Production Control form. Properly completed, it gives an accurate record of what has been done in each store. It tells the hours worked by individuals in a crew and an accounting of the shopping money issued, spent, and returned.

Bal.	Sig.	$ On Hand A.M.			$ 200	Total Ent.	
10.08	mD	Additional $ 400					
8.50	BO	Total Start			$ 600	Total Tests 29	
39.35	CR					Per	
		Total	Mdse. Spent		$542.07	Diem	
57.93		Balance Forward			$ 57.93	Itemize Exp. — Reverse Side	

Store				Entries	T	Total
Case #	2.89		7.82	10.71		
Feb. 9, 1978	4.16			4.16	3	29
Boyd's			3.29	3.29		
West County	7.05		11.11	18.16		542.01
Case #						
Case #						
Case #						

Firm _____ Store No _____ Case No _____

Address _____ City _____ State _____

Date _____ Time _____ am
                              pm Opr _____ Report No _____

Name
Number
Letter _____

Reg loc/no: _____

Reg read: _____

Sex _____ Age _____

Other cust/oprs/sales people: _____

Height _____ Weight _____

Build _____

Eyes _____ Nose _____

PAYMENT MADE										Trans No. ___
	$20	$10	$5	$1	50¢	25¢	10¢	5¢	1¢	
1. Pur										
2. Pur										Trans No. ___

Teeth _____

DESCRIPTION OF TRANSACTION

Complexion _____

Hair color _____

How combed _____

Glasses _____

Jewelry _____

Other _____

Figure 10-2. Sample shopping investigation report.

Salespersons Appearance:

_____ Well groomed

_____ Passible

_____ Average

_____ Unimpressive

_____ Unkempt

_____ Other

Salespersons Attitude:

_____ Enthusiastic

_____ Pleasant

_____ Routine

_____ Indifferent

_____ Antagonistic

_____ Served promptly

_____ Suggested other items

_____ Offered a 'thank you'

_____ Other

PURCHASES MADE

Vehicle Surveillance

The ability to conduct successful moving surveillance with today's varied traffic conditions is an art. Good "tail" men must have the ability to perform successfully in all types of conditions, whether it is expressway driving, downtown traffic conditions, interstate highway travel, or rural country roads. It becomes readily apparent that only expert drivers can master the art of successful vehicular surveillance. Persons who are knowledgeable in this area would agree that the best tail men are often to be found employed as operatives for private detective agencies which specialize in marital investigations. Some of these expert drivers are successful in maintaining weeks of tailing of male subjects who have been alerted beforehand to the strong possibility that such a surveillance may exist. Nevertheless, in spite of the evasive maneuvers which may be attempted by the subject who anticipates a surveillance, these tail men are more often successful than not.

For the beginning investigator, training in the art of vehicular surveillance is absolutely necessary. In surveillance work the subject may become "burned"; that is, suspicious or aware of the fact that he is under surveillance, without being able to pinpoint any particular agent. When the term "burned" is used in connection with an agent, it is synonymous with being "made" or identified by the subject. In this case, the agent's usefulness on the assignment is at an end.

As many evasive tactics as there are to throw off a surveillance, there is an equal number of tactics that can be employed to reduce the chances of burning the subject of the tail. As many of these tactics as possible should be demonstrated to the beginner, and from there his own imagination and experience at this type of work will further expand his abilities. Such training is not unlike the defensive driving courses taught by some of the major automobile insurance companies. Because the scope of this text does not permit an extensive discussion of vehicular tactics, consideration is confined to general points which must be borne in mind by the director of any surveillance operation.

The Surveillance Vehicle and Equipment. Rental cars are generally considered to be the best choice for vehicle surveillance. For a surveillance involving more than one person per vehicle, a four-door sedan is preferable to a two door, as the passenger can move to the rear seat to enable a different "picture" to be presented to the subject of the surveillance. The vehicle should be chosen carefully so as not to be conspicuous in color. On surveillance running a number of days, cars should be switched with the rental agency on a daily basis if at all possible. Some rental agencies will be amenable to maintaining a weekly rate in spite of the daily changes of automobiles, especially if full-sized sedans are being used.

Items kept in the surveillance vehicle should include changes of outer clothing such as caps, hats, and a reversible jacket or topcoat. Surveillance cars should also contain a pair of good quality binoculars as well as a movie or still camera equipped with telephoto lens. A closed container for liquids is necessary for relief of personal needs during car surveillances that will run an indefinite number of hours. A newspaper should also be present in the vehicle to enable the operative to have cover for his camera work and also to provide a cover for himself when parked. A person appearing to read a newspaper in an automobile draws far less attention than someone who appears to be doing nothing except sitting.

Some agencies of the federal government, along with private agencies which use automobiles regularly for tail jobs, have made certain modifications in the automobile lights. For instance, by the use of interior switches, either the left or the right headlight can be shut off, or both lights can be kept on. These various combinations, of course, add to the number of different pictures presented to the subject's rearview mirror. Interior lights should also be modified to the extent of taping down the spring buttons found in the door panels so that the lights do not come on when the doors are opened. A good investigator should never remove the bulb from the interior dome light; the dome light must be kept in operating condition, for reasons explained later.

Risks in Automobile Surveillance. In training the new agent, considerable time should be spent in attempting to inculcate in him an understanding of when it is permissible to take chances and when it is not. Any successful automobile surveillance of necessity involves a certain amount of risk to passengers of the car, pedestrians, and other vehicles on the street. These risks are further increased when it becomes necessary to violate traffic laws such as running stop signs and red lights or to speed excessively. On a long-term tailing assignment, it may be highly desirable to minimize the taking of such chances, even though the chances of losing the subject are thereby increased. It would probably be reasonable to state that maximum traffic violations would be permissible only in the event that the agent knew the "buy" had occurred or was about to take place, or that contraband was being transported to a specific location. Only at a time like this can it be justifiably said that it is not affordable to lose the tail.

Multiple-Auto Surveillance.   Obviously, the most difficult car tails are those which involve subjects who own powerful automobiles and are high-speed drivers. The high-speed driver is enough of a hazard on the road, and for this reason the surveillance director has to exercise judgment on how a successful tail job can be accomplished. For the successful tailing of such a subject, multiple automobiles must be used—a minimum of two and possibly three or four, all with adequate radio communication. This could involve a strategy of several of the cars leapfrogging with the subject, running parallel streets, or even a combination of both plus other strategies. In attempting to determine a regular route of travel of such a high-speed driver, it may be prudent for the director to utilize a number of days of surveillance, forfeiting the loss of the subject's car each day but at the same time gaining additional distance information on the subject's regular route of travel.

For the department or agency that engages in a heavy volume of vehicular surveillances, there are now devices on the market that can be attached beforehand to the subject vehicle to emit a radio signal. This, of course, requires a combination receiver and direction finder in one of the tail vehicles. The small beeper device is easily planted on a target vehicle and becomes extremely useful when visual contact with the vehicle has been lost.

Truck Tails.   Generally speaking, truck tails are much easier than automobile tails and in corporate security work are probably the more prevalent of the two. Because of their size and unusual markings, trucks are much easier to keep in sight than automobiles. One thing that the beginning agent must be aware of is the large sideview mirrors that are used with regularity by all truck drivers. For instance, in making a right-angle turn, the tail car should always make a much wider turn so as to keep out of view of the particular sideview mirror involved. On the other hand, because sideview mirrors represent the only means of viewing to the rear for the truck driver, there is also an advantage for the agent. This advantage lies in a visual dead spot immediately behind the truck, out of view of both sideview mirrors. This of course involves tailgating, and a high degree of driver capability is required to avoid an accident. However, in heavy downtown traffic conditions this often represents the only way to stay with the truck at various intersections and through traffic signals.

In corporate security work, most truck surveillances are of company trucks that regularly make deliveries or pickups. Accordingly, these trucks generally follow a prescribed route, and it is often possible on any given day to be able to determine beforehand which stops are to be made by the driver. Often the surveillance agent will make a dry run of the route beforehand to study traffic conditions, special turns, bridges, turn offs, etc. In making the dry run, the agent also has the opportunity to spot various locations along the route that can be used in his own tactics to minimize his exposure to a burn.

Burning the Subject. In both car and truck tails, one of the biggest problems the new agent must overcome is that of mental attitudes. All tail men would readily agree that early in their careers they have experienced the feeling that they have burned the subject and that the subject is aware of the tail. Experience has shown, however, that this suspicion is usually unfounded and the subject has not in fact been burned. In case after case, experienced tail men will point out that even though they had become convinced that the subject was aware of the tail, later interrogation brought out the fact that he was never aware of being followed. Only the director of a surveillance operation can keep this phenomenon in balance and be able to temper the agent's mental attitude.

As a rule of thumb, the subject who is actually burned will usually resort to illogical or seemingly pointless driving tactics in order to confirm in his own mind the probability of a tail. It is at this point that the agent must drop the tail immediately. The very dropping of the tail will confuse the subject further, as he is unable to confirm his initial suspicion. If the tail is not dropped, then the next logical maneuver on the part of the suspect would be evasive driving tactics which would tend to lose the tail.

Foot Tails

Unlike vehicular tails, which must constantly consider the picture being presented to a rearview mirror, foot tails are more concerned with simply keeping the subject in sight and using common sense so as not to burn the case.

In a foot tail, the agent must be prepared for almost any contingency. He should always have ample change in his pocket to buy a newspaper or magazine and to make phone calls. Also, he must possess sufficient funds in the event that he must take public transportation or travel by taxi. Changes of appearance are also desirable on foot tails, probably even more so than in an automobile tail, as the agent is in the open and more exposed. Here again, a cap, collapsible hat, reversible top coat, sunglasses, or other eyeglasses are all props which can greatly aid the agent in maintaining his cover. More traditional disguises, such as false beards, mustaches, and wigs generally should not be adopted unless the agent is an expert in their use and the items are realistic looking.

In teaching beginning agents how to conduct foot tails, one of the tactics employed is the traditional "picking a spot" on the rear of the subject and concentrating on that spot when following in crowded conditions. Reflections in storefront windows can also be used, but at the same time the agent should be aware that an astute subject who suspects a tail will also use the same window angles and reflections to confirm his supicions.

The agent should always keep his subject in sight and should attempt to remain closely behind him in crowded areas. If there are not too many people in the area at the time, then the agent must drop back possibly to half a block or more. If the street is virtually deserted, then the agent should do the tailing from the opposite side of the street and to the rear. If there are other pedestrians in the area, the agent should attempt to use other people as his cover.

Hand signals are usually more preferable in closeup foot tails. Any signals that are used with a second or possibly a third agent should be worked out in advance so that everyone on the tail team is thoroughly familiar with this means of communication. A newspaper, in hand, is a must for any foot tail as it can be used to emphasize hand signals and also can be used as a cover for the agent when he is observing the subject in a stationary position. A small hole in the newspaper is not discernible from a distance, but will give the agent ample field of vision.

Another tactic used by suspicious subjects is that of "rounding," which simply means making an abrupt U-turn on the sidewalk and retracing one's steps. The purpose of this, of course, is to attempt to confirm the existence of a tail. In such an event, the agent has little choice but to continue straight ahead, at least until the opportunity presents itself to turn a corner or to enter a store as a shopper would. In any event, during such a rounding operation, or on a public conveyance, or at any other time, the agent should always avoid eye contact with the subject. For some reason, eye contact more than anything else will tend to confirm the existence of a tail in the subject's mind.

When tailing the subject into a building with an elevator, the agent should attempt to get on the same elevator with the subject. The standard technique is to exit the elevator one floor above the subject and then, using the stairs, determine which room was entered by the subject.

In *The Big Brother Game*, Scott R. French (1975) makes the point that if the subject enters a restaurant and it is determined that he is not attempting to leave by the rear door the agent should be prepared to go inside and sit where he can be observed. If the subject suddenly boards a bus, French states that the agent should make every effort to board the same bus. As French points out, the subject may quickly leave the bus before it departs in an attempt to induce the agent to jump off and thus blow his cover. This simply points up the need for more than one agent on the tailing assignment. If possible, the agent should be backstopped by an automobile surveillance. All the possibilities that French attempts to cover point up the need for more than one agent on the assignment. French is in agreement with me that agents should always have a point of contact in the event that they become lost or separated. There must be someone at a telephone number who can relay messages and attempt to get the agents back together again. This is quite common in any tailing assignment, whether it be foot tails or automobile tails, and constitutes an absolute necessity if the case is of any importance whatsoever.

Report Writing

The format used for report writing on a surveillance case is quite different from that used by the undercover agent given in Chapter 8. In two-man car tails, the passenger, in addition to being the look-out and an additional pair of driving eyes for the driver, should also be charged with keeping the report. A typical surveillance report is basically a log, in chronological order, of the happenings of the day. It is somewhat more difficult to maintain during a foot tail as, obviously, the agents on the street are not able to stop and make notations on paper while tailing the subject. Often, their combined memories will be the only thing that can be used to construct a report of the day's happenings.

For the benefit of the recruit or student, we present a sample of a surveillance report in Figure 10.3.

STATIONARY SURVEILLANCE

Hotel Surveillance

Hotel surveillances are probably among the most difficult to maintain successfully. Larger hotels give more cover for the agents, but on the other hand also make it more difficult to locate the subject. Smaller hotels, conversely, offer little or no cover for the agent but do make it easier to spot the subject. If the subject is not known to the agents by sight, then obviously they must work with a photograph. Since the subject's appearance may have changed since the photo was taken, the task may seem almost impossible.

The attitude of most first-class hotels is one of noncooperation in the surveillance of their guests. However, it is often possible for the director of such a surveillance, using personal friendships and contacts, to at least gain the passive cooperation of the hotel security chief. By "passive cooperation" we mean that

To: J. Kirk Barefoot
From: Operative # 31
Re: Arrow, Atlanta, — Special Investigation

Tues, 6/3/80

5:30 PM	Operative secured vantage point in telephone booth across from subject's apartment house main entrance, 252 Park Avenue.
5:48 PM	Subject arrived at residence driving 1979 Ford Mustang, license #261 MCY. Subject parked in the apartment house garage, then proceeded to his apartment.
6:18 PM	Subject looked out his front window.
6:21 PM	Subject came to main entrance of apartment house, looked around and then returned to his apartment.
7:11	Lights in subject's apartment turned on.
7:30 PM	Eastside Market, located adjacent to subject's apartment house, closed for evening.
8:17 PM	Lights in subject's apartment turned off.
8:19 PM	Subject appeared at apartment house main entrance and proceeded west on Park Avenue on foot. Subject entered Gloria's liquor store. Operative secured vantage point across the street at bus stop.
8:35 PM	Subject exited store not carrying any parcels, and proceeded down Park Avenue to Rhone Street where he entered the Big D Jewelry store, located on the corner of Rhone and Park.
8:52 PM	Subject exited store carrying one small package. Subject returned directly to his residence walking at a very fast pace.
8:54 PM	Lights in subject's apartment turned on. Operative returned to previous vantage point.
9:47 PM	Diamond Co., taxicab 406 arrived at subject's apartment house and immediately departed after letting its fare off.
10:08 PM	Subject's apartment lights turned off.
11:00 PM	Operative discontinued surveillance and returned to residence.

Respectfully submitted
Operative # 31

Figure 10-3. Sample surveillance report.

the agents themselves will not be harrassed by the hotel security staff even though the security staff does nothing to aid the agents in their work.

On rare occasions, it may be possible for agents to rent a room directly across the hall or at either side of the subject's room. In this way, the job becomes much easier. With radio communication, the agents are in a position to watch the comings and goings of the subject and to be able to pick up on the street surveillance at the hotel entrance. If it is not possible to gain access to a nearby room, the agents must resort to frequent trips past the subject's room, listening for sounds (or the lack thereof) from within the room, and plugging the door. "Plugging" the door means the insertion in the door jamb of a match, toothpick, thread, or other small inconspicuous item that will drop from place when the door is opened.

Use of Vans, Campers, and Buildings

Setting up a surveillance in a business district is usually an easy matter. Even if parking considerations are a problem, the initial point of contact can be handled by one agent on foot with radio communication to the backup surveillance. In a residential neighborhood, the point of pickup for the surveillance team can become a problem. Not only are neighbors apt to become alarmed and call the police at the sight of a strange vehicle parked in a residential neighborhood; they may very well become suspicious to the point that loose conversation will eventually find its way to the suspect and alert him to the surveillance.

If an automobile must be used in a residential neighborhood, the surveillance director may decide that he will have to accept the possibility of suspicion on the part of the neighbors. But at least he can attempt to divert the direction of that suspicion. For example, the common tendency is to suspect that the location being watched is in front of the surveillance vehicle, in the direction toward which the agent or agents appear to be facing. In other words, the surveillance director can present this type of a picture to neighborhood residents, when in fact the agents are watching a pickup point to the rear of the surveillance vehicle via the use of sideview and rearview mirrors.

The optimum solution to residential surveillance is the use of a surveillance van or camper type vehicle. After a day or two, such a vehicle parked in a residential neighborhood draws absolutely no attention. Most of the neighbors conclude that it belongs to some visiting friends or relatives of a local resident. The use of well-equipped surveillance vans has gained in popularity in recent years, especially in corporate security departments. One large mail-order house with numerous retail outlets across the country is reported to have about fifteen of these vehicles in use. Although vans are generally not desirable for a moving surveillance, especially of automobiles, they seem to be the perfect answer to the need for cover on a stationary surveillance. Campers easily serve the same purpose; the only drawback is that there is generally no direct means of access from the inside of the camper to the cabin of the truck.

In some business districts, where a long-term stationary surveillance is desirable, it is often possible to take an informal rental of a small store or unused office. Most rental agents will often agree to the temporary rental of such a unit, especially where the transaction is handled by cash. In this type of situation, the security agent must be alert to the possibility that the rental agency may show the premises for possible legitimate leasing. The surveillance agent's furnishings, therefore, should be kept to an absolute minimum.

The use of a proper cover for a stationary foot surveillance, such as would be maintained during a buy, is only limited by one's imagination. Here, the cover could easily take the form of a small construction project, street cleaners, taxicab drivers, fisherman at a dockside, sidewalk distributors of leaflets or flyers, or any other suitable arrangement.

Coordination with Police

The question of how far to bring the local police into a private investigation can be a thorny one indeed. The problem arises because the police, in their efforts to do a proper job of patrolling, are bound to come into contact with stationary surveillance teams or may simply respond to telephone complaints from local residents. Under no circumstances should members of a surveillance team ever reveal to squad car personnel the target of their surveillance. Normally, it should be sufficient for the agents to identify themselves and state the fact that they are on a surveillance but are not at liberty to reveal the person against whom the surveillance is directed. In some small rural communities it may be advisable for the investigator not to show any official identification but to present, instead, his driver's license and give some pretext for his presence that may satisfy the patrolman.

If the security executive decides initially that the local chief or other high-ranking police official can be trusted, then an arrangement could be worked out whereby the surveillance members would simply state to the responding patrolman, "We are on a special project, with which Chief Jones is thoroughly familiar." This, of course, is not completely satisfying to the patrolman, but on the other hand he will usually think twice before challenging a statement that his own chief is privy to the situation.

One of the problems that comes about through the activities of the police patrol is the fact that in stopping the surveillance agents, the police view them as suspicious persons who are loitering in the area and may require them to get out of the vehicle and undergo a search. They may even call for an additional backup unit with the intention of removing the agents from the area to police headquarters for further questioning. Such activity tends to attract the attention of neighbors in the community and, of course, makes it impossible to use that location again.

In a large police department, prior arrangements can sometimes be made through a high-ranking commanding officer so that instructions can be issued to the patrolman on the beat that a surveillance car with private agents is going to be positioned in the area of a particular block. The block so designated may not be the target of the surveillance itself but an adjoining block; even though a certain amount of suspicion is created on the part of the local residents, it will not be apt to filter back to the suspect.

Experience has shown that when agents are stopped by a police car for speeding, upon displaying proper credentials and explaining to the officer that they are on a tail job involving a larceny, in most cases they will be allowed to proceed without a citation being issued. Here again, the agents should not reveal the type of vehicle which is being tailed, for there is really no need for this; if the officer presses for this information, it is only because of his personal curiosity.

If the surveillance agents are on a stationary stake-out of a location and they are approached at night by a police officer, their first act should be to turn on the interior lights of the car. Most police officers are extremely wary of approaching one or more occupants in a parked car at night and usually do so only when they have unholstered their weapons or at least removed the safety snap from the holster. The sudden appearance of an interior light in the automobile tends to reduce the anxiety of the approaching officer and convey the message that the agents are legitimate and that everything is open and aboveboard.

Communications and Special Equipment

Coordinating with either inside or street undercover agents, the tail men should work out in advance a contact point whereby messages can be relayed via telephone. Often the undercover agent may become aware of last-minute changes in the suspect's planning, and unless a prearranged line of communication is set up, he will be unable to convey this information to the surveillance agents. The undercover agent may also be necessary to identify certain suspects in the case. This, of course, has to be worked out in advance with the surveillance personnel so that they may pick up the suspect. (As used in surveillance work, the term pickup is not to be confused with its use as a synonym for apprehension. It simply denotes the beginning of a tail job of a particular subject at a specific location.)

Prior to the advent of modern radio equipment, hand signals were often the only way to accomplish the leapfrog concept of multiple-vehicle surveillance. Today, nationwide companies are able to obtain designated wavelengths for the use of UHF radio equipment. A good radio communication consultant is really the key to the solution of radio problems and their legality anywhere in the country. One major corporation has been able to secure a radio license covering every major location point within its industrial complex in the United States. This enables its corporate security department to move from locale to locale and still use its UHF radio equipment legally.

Earlier, reference was made to the use of a specially equipped surveillance van. A number of security departments have purchased stock vans from major auto manufacturers and modified them for their own use. If such a van is to be disguised in some way, then proper consideration should be given to the van's cover. For example, the van may have signs describing it as belonging to an industrial testing company, an engineering survey company, a pollution study firm, etc. If such cover is used and signs are affixed to the van, then the cover should be complete with telephone numbers that answer and identify themselves as an answering service.

The interior of the van should be pretty much tailor-made to the needs of the operation but should contain proper camera equipment, binoculars, chemical toilet, and food and beverage storage which would enable the agent to remain in the van for at least several days. Obviously, this would predicate the equipping of the van with a folding cot, a small table for writing reports, and other emergency equipment.

An innovation that has been made available for surveillance vans is a type of periscope which enables the occupants of the van not only to observe their target but also to make use of their photographic equipment through the periscope. Lacking a periscope, the van can also be rigged with black-out curtains on all windows except the one being used for observation. This reverse lighting effect enables the occupant to view outward through a curtain of linen composition but makes it virtually impossible for someone on the outside to see inside.

SUMMARY

Obviously, not every case lends itself to successful conclusion through the use of the various surveillance techniques. On the other hand, there are always a certain percentage of cases which can only be completed in a proper fashion through stake-outs and surveillance. A command of the intricacies of the art of surveillance is an indication of the overall ability of the security executive.

11

Conclusion

In this text, I have endeavored to give the reader insight into some of the entry-level duties for a young person just entering the security field.

Unfortunately, I have encountered a number of graduating seniors in criminal justice and industrial security programs who felt that because of their educational background they should be eligible for junior management positions in either a security firm or in a corporation. Along with this, these same graduating students had absolutely no desire to work in some of the beginning positions such as undercover agent, tail man, store detective, or guard.

Some of these positions are absolutely necessary to create the successful cases that mark the career of the top security executive. Furthermore, unless a security executive has had actual experience in these various entry-level duties, there is no way that he can ever be effective in teaching this material to other young people. Consequently, there will always be something essential lacking in a security director's complete understanding of his own business if he has not engaged in these activities.

I take pride that I have personally worked at all four of the above positions during my career, and recognize that they are absolutely essential to maintaining the momentum of a successful security program. Furthermore, in being familiar with the problems encountered by agents in these beginning assignments, I feel that I can be a better leader and teacher of my personnel than would otherwise be possible.

Bibliography

Ackerman, E.C. "Mike". *Street Man*. New York: Writers Alliance, 1976.

Astor, Saul D. Undercover investigation: A view from the grass roots. *Security World* September 1969.

Anderson, Ronald A. *Wharton's Criminal Law and Procedure*. Rochester, N.Y.: Rochester Lawyers Cooperative Publishing Co., 1957.

Barefoot, J. Kirk. *The Polygraph Story*. Linthicum Heights: American Polygraph Association, 1974.

Barefoot, J. Kirk. *Employee Theft Investigation*. Boston: Butterworth Publishers, 1979.

Caesar, Gene. *Incredible Detective*. Englewood Cliffs, N.J.: Prentice-Hall, 1968.

Carlson, John Roy. *Undercover*. New York: Dutton, 1943.

Cevetic, Matthew. *The Big Decision*. Los Angeles: published 1959.

Donovan, James B. *Strangers on a Bridge*. London: Martin Seckler & Warburg Ltd., 1964.

French, Scott R. *The Big Brother Game*. Secaucus, N.J.: Lyle Stewart, Inc., 1975.

Greene, Robert W. *The Sting Man*. Dutton: New York, 1981.

Heffron, Floyd N. *The Officer in the Courtroom*. Springfield, Ill.: Thomas, 1955.

Hunt, Morton M. Private eye to industry. *Harpers Magazine*, November 1961.

Johnson, James F., and Miller Floyd. *The Man Who Sold the Eiffel Tower*. Garden City: Doubleday, 1961.

Lubash, Arnold H. Case of the phony gangster (entrapment). *New York Times*, February 4, 1973.

Motto, Carmine J. *Undercover*. Springfield, Ill.: Thomas, 1971.

Possony, Stefan T. *The World Book Encyclopedia*, 50th Anniversary ed., 1966, vol. 6, p. 285.

Reynolds. E. Stanley. *Undercover Investigations Curtail Dishonesty*. Advance Industrial Security Information Service.

Schorr, Bert. More companies hire secret agents to spot stealing, malingering. *Wall Street Journal*, August 15, 1961.

Schultz, Donald O., and Loran A. Norton. *Police Operational Intelligence*, Springfield, Ill.: Thomas, 1968.

Security Letter, New York, February 16, 1982.

Smith, Lawrence D. *Counterfeiting*. New York: Norton, 1944.

Steven, Stewart. *The Spymasters of Israel*. New York: Macmillan 1980.

U.S. Department of Commerce. *The Economic Impact of Crimes Against Business*. February 1972.

Vizzini, Sal (with Oscar Fraley and Marshal Smith). *Vizzini*. Pinnacle Books, and Arbor House Publishing Co., 1973.

Walsh, Timothy J., and Richard J. Healey. *Protection of Assets Manual*. Santa Monica: Insurors Press, 1974.

Wesker, Rand S. Stationary surveillance. *Security Industry & Product News*, April 1981.

Index